MARTIN HAWES

Cracking open the nest egg

upstart press

A catalogue record for this book is available from the National Library of New Zealand

ISBN 978-1-990003-46-2

An Upstart Press Book

Published in 2021 by Upstart Press Ltd

26 Greenpark Road, Penrose

Auckland 1061

New Zealand

Reprinted 2022

Text © Martin Hawes 2021

The moral right of the author has been asserted.

Design and format © Upstart Press Ltd 2021

All rights reserved. No part of this publication may be reproduced or transmitted in any form or by any means, electronic or mechanical, including photocopying, recording, or any information storage and retrieval system, without permission in writing from the publisher.

Designed by Nick Turzynski, redinc. book design, www.redinc.co.nz

Printed by Printlink Ltd, New Zealand

The views and opinions expressed in this book are for informational purposes only, and do not constitute personalised financial advice. Before making any financial decisions, you should consult a financial advice provider. Disclosure information relating to Martin Hawes as a Financial Advice Provider can be viewed at www.martinhawes.com.

Contents

Preface: The $7.6m problem 5
Introduction 12

Section 1 — Planning for your best retirement . . . 26
Chapter 1: What's the Plan? 27
Chapter 2: Spending in Retirement 43
Chapter 3: Making your Money Last as Long as you do . . . 58
Chapter 4: Your Drawdown Rate 76
Chapter 5: Other Sources of Income 96
Chapter 6: The House 106

Section 2 — How to Invest in Retirement 120
Chapter 7: The Science of Investing in Retirement 121
Chapter 8: Asset Classes and Risk Management 139
Chapter 9: Investing and Getting Help 153

Afterword 178
Glossary 180
Index 191

Preface: The $7.6 million problem

My clients had sold the farm. The morning after settlement they got up and looked at their bank account; the balance was $7,595,777.43. Now, you might think that such a bank account balance would occasion great joy, an opportunity to drink Champagne for breakfast and to head to the mall or a travel agent.

In fact, my clients felt no joy at all — their primary emotions were fear and worry. They were looking at a very big number and this number represented everything they had. The result of their life's work was represented by that number on the screen — and they felt vulnerable.

To a couple who had worked hard on just one thing throughout their lives, the big number did not seem real: they had swapped a very real farm for a flickering electronic signal with a number many times larger than they had ever seen before. They knew they had to do something with this large, literally unbelievable number. They knew they could not leave it with the bank: not only was it paying a pathetic amount of interest, but they wondered whether the bank was safe.

What were they going to do with this money? How could they keep it safe? How could they get an income from it? How long would it last? With all the investment options (and all the different, competing advice they were getting from neighbours, friends and family) they knew they had exchanged a bunch of farming problems, which they knew about, for a whole bunch of new problems they knew nothing about.

Even worse was the growing realisation that there was nothing they could do with this money that was perfectly safe. Shares were scary, rental property was a lot of work (and very reliant on keeping tenants) and they did not understand bonds. Even banks could occasionally go broke.

They met with a couple of financial advisers from the city but they both seemed to speak a different language and, anyway, they seemed to care more about what they knew and what they could do rather than what a couple of newly rich farmers wanted to do with their lives.

Selling the farm and moving into town had seemed such a good idea a few months ago. Now they thought it would be much easier to worry about drought, wool prices and fence repairs than their brand new $7,595,777.43 problem.

This is an extreme example of what is happening around the country at the moment. Certainly, the number is bigger than usual, and most of us would think that $7,595,777.43 is not a bad problem to have! However, extreme though this example is (and it is nearly a true story), there are many people of retirement age who are looking at their nest egg — they've come into some cash (whether from downsizing the house, cashing in KiwiSaver, receiving an inheritance, or selling the business) and are now dealing with the biggest amount of cash they have seen in their lives, and ever will see — and they know there is not another egg in the nest!

This is all the money you are ever going to have — you have to use it well because, if you mess it up, you are not going to go back and spend another 40 years to hatch another.

$7,595,777.43 is a large number but you could take away one

or two 0s and you still get left with the same set of problems. What do you do with the money you have planned to give you the retirement you want? How do you take an income? How long will the money last?

After all, you have spent years sitting on your nest egg, caring for it, and hoping that it will grow. However, there comes a time when all care is put aside, and you have to take a hammer to it and crack it open.

A tsunami of baby boomers

That wave of baby boomers is now cresting and breaking into retirement. Long predicted, this tsunami is now with us and is rolling up a beach seemingly bare of investment options. In fact, the baby boomers, who still complain about paying 20+ percent on their mortgages in the 1980s, now find themselves trying to fashion a living from their savings at exactly the time interest rates are at record lows. At the same time as interest rates are low, we have very highly priced shares and property with poor dividend and rental yields.

We have a problem: baby boomers were always told they needed to save for retirement. By and large they did this, and many have now got to retirement age with nest eggs of varying size (yes, a few have $7,595,777.43 but more likely the amount will be around $250,000). However, regardless of the final amount, they have arrived at retirement at a time when investment looks anything but easy — interest rates are low, and they have few ideas on how these nest eggs might usefully give them a retirement income safely.

Most of the financial literacy effort has been on teaching how to build a nest egg rather than how to use that nest egg for income.

In my investment advisory practice, I have seen multiple examples of poor investment behaviour. As a response to the pinch that these new or prospective retirees find themselves in, some have adopted a strategy of putting all their money in just one asset. For example they have purchased a rental property or continued to own a business. This means that they are not diversified but instead have concentrated their funds in just one asset class. And some are not having the retirement of their dreams. They stay on in the business as they kick the retirement can down the road, to pick it up (maybe) another day.

Others have ratcheted up risk by having portfolios with more shares than they ought; with returns from bank deposits and fixed interest investments virtually non-existent, they have turned to asset classes (shares and listed property) which look expensive but are at least doing OK for the time being. Repeatedly, I see people abandon balanced portfolios for growth portfolios and funds with less fixed interest and cash, but more shares and property.

Still others have simply held on to their term deposits, regardless of the paltry returns. The minimal returns they have been getting from the bank mean that to maintain any reasonable kind of lifestyle they are required to spend more capital. This, in turn, means that they run the risk of the money running out long before they do.

Of course, many people look at their options and, shunning retirement, carry on with work. That seems safer than putting their dearly beloved nest egg at risk.

To many retirees, accumulation of wealth was easy; it is the decumulation that is now necessary that is the hard part.

Diversify, diversify, diversify

In fact, there is a solution to the problem of investing in retirement, the same solution that people should always have adopted regardless of interest rates or valuations of other investments classes: that solution is to spread your money across all investment types and to get money into a range of different industries and countries. This is a diversified portfolio.

A diversified portfolio may not make you rich, but it is the best store of wealth ever invented. You may have built your wealth by concentrating your money to just one asset or asset class (you may have owned a business or some rental properties, or you may have invested aggressively in shares), but retirement is a time to lower risk as you start to enjoy what you have. Lowering risk means diversification.

There are plenty of options for diversification but that does not make it easy to choose which one. At the time of writing, there is only one fund that is a specialist drawdown fund, a fund designed specifically for retirees to invest in and draw out their money for a regular fortnightly income. (Disclosure: I am a director and shareholder of this fund.)

Other funds can be used to hold investment capital, which is then drawn on to provide a living. Many KiwiSaver funds are suitable for this, and other managed funds are also on offer from banks and fund managers.

A lot of people in New Zealand find it hard to get good advice. There are some very good financial advisers in practice but most only take on clients who have significant amounts of money (often the minimum is $250,000, but sometimes significantly more more). Those with $7,595,777.43 will be fine — every financial adviser in the country will beat a path to those farmers' door.

But people with smaller amounts either need to go to a bank or fund manager and take advice from people who are advising on and selling only their own product. Regrettably, many people are simply left to their own devices.

All of this is complicated by the demise of the Defined Benefit superannuation scheme. These schemes, which started to be wound down in the 1990s, paid a percentage of finishing salary. Typically, employees would pay into these schemes and when they finished their careers as doctors, managers, teachers, etc., they would receive 60% of their salary until they died. These schemes were marvels of generosity — the contributions employees made went nowhere near covering the cost and left the government (in the case of public service employees) and companies (in the case of private sector employees) holding big liabilities.

Such was the cost, these Defined Benefit schemes were closed to new members. There are still plenty of people receiving them, but none is open to new members — the cost of paying a lifetime pension means no Defined Benefit scheme is ever likely to emerge again.

Now we are left to our own devices. Superannuation savings and KiwiSaver are now Defined Contribution (that is we know the amount we are contributing but not what will come out in the end). At the end of employment, we receive a lump sum according to what we have contributed, the amount that our employers may have contributed, and the investment returns that we got on the way through.

It is then our job to convert that lump sum into a pension. This job had been both so difficult and so expensive for Super schemes (with their investment experts and actuaries) that they had stopped doing it. But now we expect everyone to be able to do it themselves, without access to those actuaries and experts. That is a very big ask.

Drawdown — how much can you safely withdraw?

Given that we all have to look after our own money and investments now that there is no joining a Defined Benefit scheme, there are and will be problems. These problems of how to invest in retirement are in addition to that age-old problem of knowing how much you can reasonably draw from a portfolio. Even when retirees have invested their money well, they face the problem of figuring out how much they can take from the portfolio on a monthly or fortnightly basis so that the money will last as long as they do.

This is setting the right drawdown rate and it is critical to a good retirement. If you take too much from your portfolio, you run up against longevity risk; your money may not last as long as you do and you end up in your final years reusing tea bags and rationing the wine biscuits you eat for dinner. On the other hand, if you take too little, you forgo lifestyle — the children will benefit, at your expense, from your lower expenditure as you leave bigger inheritances.

There are two things that most people will have to do for a decent retirement:

1. You will have to invest in a diversified portfolio which, as will become clear, is no bad thing. No longer can people live on the interest from bank deposits and the likes, instead you will need to invest in a managed fund (or funds) and possibly enlist the help of a financial adviser.
2. You will need to spend not just the returns you get from investments but also some of the capital. This will mean that in retirement you will probably need to decumulate your savings, leading to smaller inheritances for the children.

This book sets out to help people with the way they should invest when the nest egg has hatched, and how they draw down from their savings to give a good retirement. These should be the best years of your life, but you need a happy fit between you and your money. Whether you have $7,595,777.43, or something more modest, you will have decisions to make.

As the reality of retirement strikes, there are a lot of people finding that although they had put some effort into accumulating a nest egg, they had never given much thought to how (and how fast) they would decumulate it. Now they need to.

Martin Hawes
October 2021

Introduction

The hardest thing to do in finance is to take a lump sum and use it to generate a good and steady income in retirement. It was always difficult but, in a world of very low interest rates, it has become even more so. For a long time, Kiwis have retired and largely used bank deposits to give them a retirement income. I doubt that this was ever a very good idea but now it is downright impossible.

In fact, it is not just interest rates that are low, but so too are dividend yields and rents. This is now at the point when few can take some capital and simply live on the income it generates. Instead, investors have to invest in a range of asset classes and draw an amount from that portfolio that allows them a good living.

The second hardest thing to do in finance is to decide how fast you will decumulate your savings, i.e. your drawdown rate. This book is really about the decumulation stage of life and the trick with this is to try to make your money last as long as you do.

Decumulation is a word that we are starting to hear more often as the baby boomers move into retirement. Most of us spend our working lives accumulating assets as we buy a house, pay off the mortgage, contribute to KiwiSaver and then, if we have done well, start to invest. All of this means that we accumulate wealth.

Come retirement, we then have to use the wealth we have accumulated to provide an income. Work stops (or at least slows down). NZ Super starts, but that is not enough to live on for most. We now need to use our accumulated wealth to plug that gap between NZ Super and the way we want to live. We need to find a way to substitute the income we had from work with the income we derive from the wealth we have accumulated.

In retirement, most people now truly decumulate as they run their capital down. Living solely on investment returns, and keeping all of your capital intact, now sits somewhere between difficult and impossible. We live longer, and a lot of people are very active in retirement (and therefore spend a lot). Unless you really do have $7,595,777.43 to live on, chances are you are not going to be able to leave a lot of your wealth to your children. You will need to start to decumulate.

It is this decumulation that is hard: not only do we have to make it last as long as we do, but we also have to watch our most precious savings decline — we have to take a hammer to our nest egg and chip away at it until it becomes next to nothing. In the decumulation stage, your wealth will gradually reduce as you eat into it. Chances are this will leave you feeling very uncomfortable about how long the money will last.

So, your decumulation needs to be set at the right rate — too fast and you will run out of money; too slow and you will have given up invaluable lifestyle during your best years. Deciding on that figure is hard.

Drawdown

The rate at which you take money from your investments is called the 'drawdown rate'. I refer to the drawdown rate throughout this book. It is about setting a withdrawal rate at the right level so that you have a good life and do not underspend, but so the money lasts.

Calculating a reasonable drawdown rate is fiendishly difficult; it depends on:
- how you invest
- the returns that you get
- the vagaries of financial markets

- your tax rate
- inflation rates
- expenditure
- expenditure changes through retirement
- how long you are likely to live
- the state of your health as you progress through retirement

Calculating the right average drawdown rate across the whole population has any number of variables (e.g. life expectancy, investment ability, expenditure patterns, etc.) that need to be calculated (or guessed) for perhaps the next 30 years. Doing this for an individual, who may (but probably will not) be average for the variables, is even more difficult and subject to error. You are a sample of one and will probably prove to be nothing like the average.

We are all different and have different plans: some will happily let the cheque to the undertaker bounce as they go out on the last dollar, whereas others will want to leave everything they ever had intact to the children. Some will want to spend up large in the early years of retirement whereas others will be more cautious. Some will look at their parents and decide they will not make old bones while others believe they will live forever.

Actuaries, a profession of very clever people who are trained to make these kinds of calculations, have worked hard over the years to come up with several rules of thumb for a drawdown rate that will suit most people. Of course, they cannot account for you as an individual — although you may live the average time, it is more likely that you will live for a longer or shorter time than average. Moreover, your expenditure may be average overall, but you may decide to spend a lot shortly after you retire, or you may decide to spend less so that you have access to better healthcare towards the end of your life.

These rules of thumb are very useful, but they are not as good as a calculation that would personalise your drawdown rate. However, few people can make these calculations themselves, unfortunately

— there are simply too many unknowns (some of which may even be unknown unknowns!) — so, in the absence of personalisation, it is best to work with the rules of thumb.

The 4% rule of thumb

Generally, drawdown rates are expressed as a percentage of the amount you have invested. For example, the most commonly used drawdown rates is known as the 4% rule. This rule means that at the beginning of retirement you can draw 4% of your portfolio to live on each year and increase this amount with inflation as you progress through retirement. If you do this, and provided your money is invested in a balanced fund (50% in shares and 50% fixed interest), the 4% rule of thumb says that your money will last for 30 years.

That would mean that if you had a balanced portfolio to the value of $500,000, in the first year you could draw $20,000 p.a. (i.e. 4%) and increase that so that your $20,000 p.a. keeps up with inflation and maintains its spending power. If you had retired at age 65, your money would last until you are aged 95.

There are several caveats with this rule. This and the other rules of thumb, regarding rates of drawdown, are discussed in chapter 4. Although these are all rules of thumb, and therefore a bit rough and ready, unless we can personalise a drawdown rate solely for you, they are the best we have to try to plan for retirement. Financial advisers will be able to refine this for you, but there will still be some unknowns (e.g. longevity, spending patterns and investment returns) and so, even when we try to personalise a drawdown rate, it will not be perfect.

Decumulation

As the baby boomers retire en masse, decumulation is becoming the word of the day, and I now know few people who plan to leave a lot of their investment capital behind as inheritances. In fact, the great majority of people I talk to plan to leave the house for the children, if they can, but to spend both investment returns and the capital itself in retirement. This seems to me to be a significant shift over the last 10 years or so.

Letting the cheque to the undertaker bounce

Decumulation will inevitably have an impact on what you leave behind. Our children may be enjoying very low interest rates on their mortgages at the moment, but the flipside of this is that we as parents are having to spend what might have been our children's inheritances. And many of us are going to make retirement the time of our life, go out on the last dollar, and let the cheque to the undertaker bounce! Some people may try to spend just their investment returns, but when that is not enough, they will have to spend their capital as well.

I have long had an interest in this decumulation phase. My interest was piqued because there are technical aspects to making sure a portfolio is well invested, but there are also behavioural issues. This book makes a strong case for diversification in retirement (in fact, I think it essential that retirees diversify) but many people find changing the habits of a lifetime difficult. Some people have invested in a particular way (e.g. they have owned some rental properties) and do not see any need to spread their money more widely when they are older — they would prefer to hug the familiar. However, you may be retired a long time, and anything can happen over that time. You need to own different asset classes so, regardless of what the economic weather, you always have some investments that will do well.

The great mismatch

In a world of low interest rates, we must use volatile assets (shares and listed property) to meet our demand for a steady income. This is a mismatch; normally you would not try to get a steady income from a portfolio that contained a lot of volatile assets. However, because interest rates are so low, there is no alternative — you must have some shares and listed property in your portfolio or fund. It would be easy if we could match our requirement for a sufficient and steady income with an investment which was sure to provide that, but such an investment does not exist.

Unless you took a government fixed interest investment with a maturity in 30 years (which should see you out), you cannot be certain that you will get the expected return. Such an investment is, of course, not a starter because at the time of writing, the interest rate would be just 2.3% and, after tax, this is unlikely to even keep up with inflation — after (say) 10 years, your nominal income would be the same, but its spending power would be diminished.

And so, we have to add other investments (especially shares and listed property) to give higher returns. Unfortunately, but inevitably, these come with volatility. Investors only get paid for taking on risk — and the more risk they assume, the better they are paid (i.e. the better the returns).

This book does not set out to know the unknowns — no one knows what investment returns will be next year, nor can they know when they will die. Instead, this book tries to manage these unknowns and mitigate their effects, and to manage volatility and the variation of returns, which come from a portfolio that has shares and listed property in it.

All this difficulty (good investing and prudent drawdown rates) comes at a time when you should be looking forward with pleasure to your 20 good summers. However, people often face a worrisome set of decisions. These decisions are exacerbated by two things:
1. You have to work your way through a tightly woven cloth of vested interest. There are competing claims and opinions, and this all comes at you in brand new language, which you may never have learned.
2. Everything is on the line. In retirement there is no time to

rectify major mistakes — one false move and everything you have worked for can be lost.

Little wonder that people are nervous when they move to crack open their nest egg.

Diversification

Throughout our working lives there are all sorts of people giving advice or commentating on saving for retirement — people telling us about property investment, KiwiSaver, how to save, etc. However, although there is plenty of advice on accumulation, there is very little comment or advice on managing your money in retirement.

And so, retirees cast around for options. With the easy option of putting their money in the bank and living off the interest completely gone, they look for alternatives.

My strongest advice for people who are going into retirement is that they diversify their savings. They may have made their money through a single asset type (perhaps their own business or a property portfolio) but the thing that made the money is not necessarily the best way to hold on to the money. When you are young you can afford to take risk — and so you may have put all your eggs in one basket. With a bit of luck, all will be good. However, when you come to retirement you cannot push out risk — you cannot bet everything on just one thing.

It is always tempting to stay with the familiar, but there is no single asset class that will hold your money safe through all the years of retirement. A big part of this book is about investing your retirement savings for income — and diversifying is a key theme.

By the time you have got to retirement, the get-rich game is over. Now is the time to play stay-rich. And there is only one place you should look to put your money in retirement — a diversified portfolio.

Get some help

I think most people should have their investments managed for them rather than the old idea of taking a DIY approach. Having your investments managed for you could take one of two forms: either you invest by way of a managed fund (or, perhaps a range of managed funds) or you have a financial adviser put together a portfolio and manage it for you.

Investment is a lot more complicated than it used to be; there are more options for your investments and more choices to be made, meaning that there is little scope for DIY investors who are not very well informed and not prepared to put a great deal of time into investment strategy, investment selection and investment management. I have looked at many DIY portfolios over the years and found them lacking in many respects, and I now look at chat sites used by many young investors who have just come into investment. I am often appalled by the lack of knowledge.

Although DIY may be reasonable for younger people with smaller amounts of money that they can afford to lose, it is completely unreasonable for a retired person whose portfolio is their means to living a good life.

It is likely that a professionally managed fund (i.e. KiwiSaver, a drawdown fund, or other managed fund) will have a performance that is better, and this superior performance should more than compensate for the fees you pay. I recently read of a US study by fund manager Vanguard which showed that over a 25-year period an adviser-managed portfolio averaged 8%, while a self-managed portfolio returned 5%. Professional management pays.

That difference would pay the fees with a lot left over, and most people I know would be better off with a professionally managed investment portfolio. This includes myself — even though I know quite a lot about investment, I do not want to spend a lot of time staring at a screen and so I now have someone investing my money for me.

The book is divided into two parts: the first concerns some of the most important planning issues. I have called this section 'Planning for your best retirement' and it covers some of the key planning issues that must be addressed. The second section of the book is called 'How to invest in retirement' and it covers the most important aspects of investing *in* retirement (which is quite different from investing *for* retirement).

Section 1 — Planning for your best retirement

It is tempting to go straight to the matters that are in the second section of this book — that is, how we should invest our money. Unfortunately, in doing this you ignore some of the big issues that need to be thought through and planned for. These planning issues are dealt with in the first six chapters which cover:

- Money management, spending capital and making the transition;
- The amount you can draw from a portfolio;
- Your levels of expenditure and, importantly, how this will change over time; and
- Consideration of housing and how that may be used to either free up some capital for more investing or how the house itself may be used for income.

All of these are important issues and can impact the quality of your retirement either positively or negatively. A good retirement requires you to think about all aspects of your finances — investment is one of these but there are other things to get right first.

Having your money run out before you do is the biggest fear of those going into retirement: people are fearful they will wake up one morning and see that their money has all been spent. The idea that this will happen suddenly and long before you are likely to die runs deep.

In fact, it seldom happens like that: people tend to underspend rather than overspend in retirement. While it is quite true that some people do make big investment mistakes in their retirements and end up with no money, this is usually because they move out of the safety of diversification. However, they seldom draw down too much and even when they do, or when markets take one of their periodic downturns, they adjust their expenditure. As such, money does not run out even though lifestyle may.

People do sometimes have to adjust their expenditure but often enough this happens naturally. As I discuss in chapter 2, our expenditure tends to decrease as we age — over the course of retirement (which may be 30 years or more) our lifestyles change and our spending patterns with it.

Whatever you want to leave behind, a lot or a little, will largely be determined by your drawdown rate — the amount of money that you take from the portfolio either as a regular amount (your monthly spend) or occasional lump sums. Although there are basic rules of thumb regarding how much you can draw out from your investments, this is a very personal thing and the rate at which you draw may need to be adjusted higher or lower from the norm, which will affect what you leave as bequests.

One of the big factors that affects your drawdown rate is how long the money needs to last — or, to put this more bluntly, when you think you are going to die. To take some extremes: if you thought you were going to die next week, you would put all your money in cash and spend like there is no tomorrow (because there is no tomorrow for you!). On the other hand, if you have retired in your fifties and believe that you could live to 105 years, you need to draw a lot less as you parsimoniously eke out your funds to make them last fifty years.

The rate at which you can draw is one of the key parts of any retirement plan and is explored in chapter 4.

Section 2 — How to invest in retirement

As noted, the second section covers some investment questions that are specific to those who are dependent on their investment capital for their income. I have already said that there is no sensible alternative to a diversified set of investments and the second section of the book assumes that you will follow that rather than adopt some kind of eccentric investment strategy.

The things covered in this section include:
- The types of investment that you will have, how they should be mixed and the importance of spreading your money far and wide;
- How to arrange your money for best effect;
- Who you should have to advise you and/or to help you build the right investment mix; and
- Risk management: the things that might befall you and what you can do about them.

I do think KiwiSaver is improving financial literacy in New Zealand — as part of the national KiwiSaver conversation, there is a lot of discussion about asset allocation and other investment topics which have arisen. However, retirees have their own investment issues. The way a 40-year-old might invest is quite different from how a 70-year-old ought to invest. I may be quite happy to see a 40-year-old invest in just one asset class (say, everything in property or everything in global shares) but I would not sit quietly and say nothing if a 70-year-old was similarly invested.

The 70-year-old cannot afford to take absolute loss. Those who are in retirement can afford some portfolio volatility; this is simply the usual ups and downs of the markets and, as I show in this book, that can be managed if you have your finances structured properly. What cannot be managed is complete loss — and that can happen if you are invested in just one asset or just one investment type.

If you have a good, diversified portfolio, you may have exposure to perhaps 1000 different securities; while some of those will struggle at times and a few may even go under, they will not all fail. If all those 1000 entities you are invested in go broke, the world is in a power of trouble.

The key thing to avoid is selling some of your investments when markets are down. This sounds unavoidable — after all, you will be drawing on the portfolio regularly and, no matter whether markets are up or down, you have to eat so will need to sell some investments. Fortunately, selling in a down market ought not always be necessary; I think it essential to hold a 'lake of cash' as I outline in chapter 3.

Volatility risk is unavoidable in any portfolio. If investors get paid for taking risk, no risk inevitably means no return. The trick is to recognise that there will be volatility and make sure that you manage it. Risk and its implications for retired investors is critical; read chapter 7.

The time of your life

Whatever your planned retirement, it should be the best of times. You have worked, saved and built a nest egg to be able to retire and now you should be able to crack open the nest egg to live life just the way you have always wanted. Your retirement should be good compensation for the time and money you gave up when you were younger. Now is the time to get on with whatever it is that you always wanted to do and make retirement the time of your life.

In my book *20 Good Summers*, I wrote of the way that time was encroaching, and, for some, it was time for a reset of life and the things that you do. That could mean going into early semi-retirement and I showed how the numbers could be worked to facilitate this much more easily than many imagined.

Now, 15 years later, for many of us complete retirement is on (or over) the horizon. That is time for another reset.

It is a big reset — and you do have to get it right. There is no chance of a practice run, no dress rehearsal to figure out what is important. You will only get one shot at this.

This book has been formed and informed by many of the hundreds of clients I have seen over the last 20 years. Most of these were going into retirement (or, at least, planning their retirements) and I have learned something from them all.

The thing I have learned most is that retirement is a big, scary leap into the unknown. I have known people to have multiple attempts at it as they have retired and then scurried back to the safety of employment several times (these are recidivist retirees, and I could name a few of them).

There are all sorts of factors that cause the fear of retirement — their social lives, their standing in the community, relationship reset, etc. This is a big change which comes at a time of life when we may no longer be any good at change.

However, the big factor that I see most often is the fear that is engendered by that transition from a regular pay cheque to having to live off their capital. Money and investment are difficult at the best of times, and these are not the best of times for all people. The idea that they now have to eke out a living by investing their money in volatile markets is enough to send many people back to work.

Yes, a new stage of life is scary. This stage could last for thirty years or longer and over that time many things will happen, both good and bad. Given that this final stage of our lives should be as good as we can possibly make it, retirement deserves some planning. This book is aimed at helping you do that and helping you make the next twenty (or thirty, or forty) summers as good as you can.

I reckon #1 — Ease your way into retirement

I may well be a fake! Past the age of retirement, I am pontificating about stopping work with no actual experience of it. I have not retired, and I have not yet even had one unsuccessful attempt at retirement as several of my friends have. Although I frequently think about retirement, I have no plans yet to do so.

I have stopped doing some of the things that used to keep me overly busy (I have ceased to give personal financial advice) and this has certainly freed up some time. However, full retirement, stopping everything, is still a step too far.

I have to admit I still find retirement scary. I have enough money; the financial side of retirement holds no terrors. And I am not frightened by the need to fill in my days. Rather, I am scared of calling an end to something which would be final. Given what I do, it would be very hard once stopped to go back and start again. Retirement would be final for me, the end of my work and contribution.

Nevertheless, even though I have not yet lived in retirement, I have watched and advised many people who are retired or retiring. I learned something from just about all of the clients I have had and even though I no longer see clients, I meet and talk retirement to people regularly.

I reckon that retirement should be done gradually, in a series of steps if possible. This not only allows you to make some of the social and family changes that are almost always necessary, but also to start to look at the expenditure your new life may require and, perhaps most importantly, to set up the investments that you will need to live on. My experience with many people is that they find portfolio investment new and scary (there can be a basic mistrust) but, when they have done it for a while, they become accustomed to it and their comfort grows.

SECTION 1 —

Planning for your best retirement

CHAPTER 1
What's the Plan?

This chapter is an overview of how to make a plan for retirement, showing how the pieces fit together. I could write for a very long time on the need for planning (repeat after me: fail to plan, plan to fail). Only some of the main issues are dealt with in detail in this chapter because others need, and are given, much more space in later chapters (e.g. drawdown rates and the important role of the house in the finances of retirement). This chapter should, therefore, be seen as putting things in context, thinking about the compromises you will probably need to make and, perhaps more than anything else, planning so that you can afford to retire and to make that retirement as good as your resources will allow.

The key things that you will need to consider (and maybe juggle) so that you will have enough income in retirement include:
- your net worth
- the amount tied up in the house
- the amount in investment capital
- your drawdown rate
- your expenditure
- other income (NZ Super, work, taking in a boarder)
- inheritances that you want to leave
- time in retirement (i.e. life expectancy)

These things make up a matrix. Each of these components can be considered and changed so that you can retire and, hopefully, retire in comfort. For example, if you cannot make the numbers work so that you can have a good retirement, you could decide to work a little, or downsize the house to a less expensive option. The work would, obviously enough, give you extra income for a number of years, and downsizing the house would mean that you would have more capital to invest, which would also give more income.

All of the items listed above (with the exception of life expectancy, which will always be the big unknown) can be varied or traded off against each other to give you the best retirement you can afford. Financial planning is always about compromise — no one can have everything — so we have to trade off one thing to have another that is more important to us. For example:

- You give up a bigger house so that you have more income to travel;
- You delay retirement so that you can have more when you do retire;
- You plan to reduce expenditure later in retirement so that you can do more in the early years of retirement;
- You increase the inheritances you will leave by reducing your drawdown rate; or
- You take in a boarder at the expense of privacy, but which allows a higher expenditure.

All of these are compromises to try to get the happiest fit for you in retirement — some may be the kinds of things that you do not *want* to do, but they are better than the alternative. No one ever said that planning for your best retirement was going to be easy!

The house and some money to invest

Ultimately, the key question for people in their fifties, sixties and seventies (and, at times, beyond) is how much investment capital you need for a good retirement. Regardless of whether you want to retire or not, you need to know whether you could retire if you needed or wanted to — and, if you do not have enough money, how much more saving you need to accumulate.

The planning process is, in large part, to see:
1. How much money you will have to invest for income; and
2. What amount you can draw from these investments or, perhaps, what amount you have to draw.

People often say things like: 'I have the house and $500,000.' What they mean by this is that the $500,000 is available for investment to give them income, and after deciding how much they plan to take from the portfolio each year, they can decide whether this is sufficient income to fund the lifestyle that they want.

Of course, you can see that there are other factors to consider and plan for (e.g. the work that you may do early in retirement, or the inheritances you may or may not leave), but the big things in the end are a right-sized house and an amount to be invested for income.

Most people work through the issues in retirement planning almost intuitively. They know the kinds of things that are important to them and the decisions that need to be made. A summary of the basic retirement planning process looks like this:

1. **Calculate your net worth.** This is everything that you own, less what you owe. It will give you a number that adds up all your assets and, after subtracting any liabilities, gives you the net amount that you are worth.
2. **Decide on how much you will have tied up in the house.** This is a personal decision and will involve consideration of many issues beyond financial ones. Nevertheless, every dollar that is in the house is one that is not invested for income and the lifestyle that this income will afford. Your total net worth includes the value of the house. Where you choose to draw the line between the house and your investment capital is a key decision that we all have to make (see chapter 6).

3. **Drawdown rate.** This is the amount that you can draw from your capital. Although I use the 4% rule for this section (it is the safest, and probably most commonly used), your drawdown rate will probably be greater than 4%. Chapter 4 of this book discusses drawdown rates.
4. **Look for all other sources of income.** Other income covers things like New Zealand Super, work, other pensions, or using a sleep-out for rental or short-term accommodation. Of course, some people work for social (rather than financial) reasons, and others may also rent out a room for the company rather than money. Nevertheless, there are a lot of people who need to work or look for other sources of income because they need the money to make a (semi-) retirement work (see chapter 5).
5. **Expenditure.** This means doing some kind of budget and, in that process, working out what is really important to you and what you might have to give up to make the budget balance. It also means considering the patterns of expenditure throughout retirement — expenditure will change over retirement, and you need to give a lot of thought to how you will live through the various stages of retirement (see chapter 2).
1. **Compare income to expenditure.** When you have added together all of your income you can then compare that to your expenditure budget. This comparison will either lead to great happiness, or mean you have to review everything again to see if you can make some adjustments so that the income and expenditure match.

How much do you have?

The first step here is to see what you have, and that means having a look at your net worth. This is a stock-take to work out how much wealth you have and what that wealth is made up of. When you have a net worth statement (the things that you own less anything you might owe) you can consider this to see how it is split between your house (and other lifestyle) assets and money that is available for investment.

A key part of this step is deciding what is 'in play' and what is not 'in play'. Things that are 'in play' are assets you would sell to add to your investment capital; those that are not 'in play' are assets you would not sell almost regardless of your circumstances. For example, you may own three paintings worth $30,000. If these were bought a couple of years ago and you are already a bit tired of them, they would certainly be 'in play' — you could sell them and put the proceeds towards your investments for increased income. However, if they were painted by your grandmother 50 years ago and the whole family loves them (they are promised to the children) then they are not 'in play'. They will not be sold under any circumstances.

Some people's houses are 'in play' as they would downsize readily enough. Others will not touch the house, neither to sell it nor remortgage using a Reverse Mortgage product. You will need to decide what might go to investment capital for income, and what will not be sold but retained for the future.

Looking forward

Once you know what you have and the value and nature of the main assets, you can start to look forward and see how much you will need for a good retirement when you stop work.

Looking at your total assets, you will need to deduct the following:
1. The amount of debt that you have (you do not want to go into retirement with debt so this needs to be repaid — see below).
2. The value of the house (or a new house if you are planning to downsize).
3. The value of any toys (camper van, boat, etc.) you plan to keep or buy.

You are the left with an amount that should be available to be invested to give you an income.

Example — working out the amount you have for investing
Karen and Phil have a net worth of $1.6 million. They have no debt.

They have decided that they will downsize the house to buy one for $900,000. They will also buy a camper van and boat, which together will total $100,000. They had also promised both their children that they would help them buy their first home; they will give each child $50,000 for a total of $100,000.

And so, their position after the purchase of a new home, purchase of the van and boat, and gifts to the children would look like this:

Net worth $1.6m
Less
House $900,000
Van and boat . . $100,000
Gifts $100,000

Investment $500,000

Repay debt

Of course, this assumes that you have no debt — I believe it a basic rule that retirees should have no borrowings. This is for two reasons:
1. Having debt adds to your cost base — you are effectively investing your funds to pay interest.
2. You are subject to the vagaries of another market — the interest rate market. As I write, interest rates are very low. However, interest rates could rise in the future (possibly quite sharply) and that would leave you very exposed.

Therefore, before you go into retirement, allocate some of your capital to repay any debt that you have. While it may be reasonable to have a little debt that will be paid off shortly (e.g. a hire purchase that is close to being repaid), it is not good to have significant debt for the medium to long term.

Income and expenditure

Once you know how much you have available to invest, your next task is to work out how much you can safely draw from the investment portfolio each year. This is the drawdown rate, and it is one of the most important decisions you will need to make to have a good retirement plan. Two chapters are devoted to this (chapters 3 and 4), where the various rules of thumb are set out and the likely consequences of drawing out particular amounts.

Whatever the drawdown rate you choose, you will need to apply that to the amount of capital that you have to see if you will have enough income to retire. For example, after you have right-sized the house, repaid debt and bought lifestyle assets you have $500,000 of investment capital. If your drawdown was going to be 4%, you would have additional income of $20,000 p.a. from your investment capital.

When you have planned your income from your investment, you can then add any other income you will receive. You will probably have NZ Super and some people may have other income from work or a micro-business (see chapter 5). You can then consider your likely expenditure and compare that to the income that you have planned. This may be a moment of great joy, or it could send you back to make some other decisions.

These other decisions may be necessary because you have realised that you will not have enough to retire. However, that should only be the start of the process as there are many things that can be changed or modified to make the numbers work and to allow for a good retirement.

It may mean that you will need to give up some things or some activities. Another alternative may be that you keep on working and don't retire until you have enough money. However, many people would find this a price too high to pay. Instead, they could be better off looking at possible adjustments to make things work. This process may need to be done multiple times.

The process should, therefore, be iterative — that is, once you have done it there is a good chance you will need to go back to it again and adjust some parts to try to get a good balance between what you have and the lifestyle you want. For example, you may have to look at the house and plan to downsize to a greater extent than first planned so that you have more capital to be invested for income.

This will often mean you need to compromise. Life is full of these kinds of compromises — you can have the travel, or you can have the bigger house, but you cannot have both. No one can have everything, and we frequently have to give up one thing so that we can have the other.

The things that you could look at to increase your income include:

- **The house.** This is probably your biggest asset, and, as such, when you are trying to make plans, it is an obvious first place to start. Although it is primarily a place to live, it can also be used for income. This additional income could come from downsizing the house — this could be hard to do but remember that each $100,000 that you can free up by downsizing will mean $4,000 of income each year (I have applied the 4% rule here). However, if you have decided to keep it, you could use a home equity release product (reverse mortgage) and draw income through that. For years (probably centuries), older people have taken in boarders (read Airbnb today) and gained income from doing that (see chapter 6).
- **Other lifestyle assets.** People go into retirement with plans to do things. They know this is their big and probably last chance to do all the things they have always wanted to do

but have not been able to because work got in the way. On retirement, people often buy things like camper vans, boats, artwork, new cars, sports gear, motorbikes, etc. Much of this stuff will be needed for the life that you want, and far be it for me to say you should not have it. What I would say is make sure that you will use these things enough to justify buying them. If not, there may be other ways of achieving the same end. For example, you may be able to rent a motorbike as it is needed or perhaps share ownership of a boat with another family. Remember as you go over and over your plans that money spent on these things directly takes from other potential lifestyle activities. Remember also that most of these things are value losers. In other words, you will not be able to sell them later in retirement for what you paid for them. Therefore, make sure that you really want them and that buying them is the only way to have use of them.

- **Work.** It always seems wrong to include work as a possible income stream in a book about retirement. After all, retirement is about saying goodbye to work. However, for those who cannot quite make the numbers work, committing to some small amount of work can allow semi-retirement, which in some cases may be as good (or nearly as good) as full retirement. A lot depends on the nature of the work. Some people hate the idea of carrying on with what they did before (a change is as good as a holiday, and they want to do something different). On the other hand, others carry on with their existing work (admittedly, at a lower level) because it is easy doing something they know. For a lot of people whether to work in retirement depends on the hours and the flexibility it comes with. People report that retirement is a busy time. ('How did we ever fit in a day job?' is a comment I often hear), and there are always things to do and places to go. Nevertheless, even a quite small amount of work can make the numbers work and offer a whole new lifestyle which can be very attractive even if it is not quite complete retirement (see chapter 5).

- **Drawdown rate.** In this chapter I have suggested that using the 4% rule (i.e. a drawdown rate of 4% of your starting investable capital each year) is a reasonable amount for most people (although as you will see later, this can vary). Using this 4% rate means that you can increase the amount you drawdown to keep up with inflation and, according to the rule, at drawdown of 4%, your money will last 30 years. However, the 4% rule is not set in stone and things can happen which mean that it does not work out perfectly (e.g. investment returns may be greater or less than expected, and the sequencing of those returns can vary). Moreover, as discussed on page 44, expenditure often does not remain the same throughout retirement — in fact, research shows that expenditure tends to be higher early in retirement but falls as people age. It may, therefore, be that you take a little more risk and draw more than 4% early in retirement as you plan to spend less later. There are also other drawdown rates that you can reasonably use, and these are outlined in chapter 4, and for a lot of people, the 6% rule would be better.
- **Other income sources.** If you are struggling to make retirement numbers work, you need to go on a hunt for other income or, perhaps, more investment capital. You will probably have NZ Super, but there may be other income streams that you can develop without too much work or capital required. These are things like a short-term rental of a room in your house or a micro-business. You may also be able to increase the amount of capital that you have invested by selling some things that you no longer use. I know several retired people who seem to spend a lot of their time on Trade Me.

Other things to factor in are:

- **Inheritance — giving.** Most retirement plans assume that you will try to spend all your investment capital and leave the house for the children. Although in my experience this is now the most common plan, there is a very wide variation. Some people would happily spend the capital they have in the house as well as run down their investment portfolios to zero (this is easy to say, but in a practical sense, harder to do). Others want to leave everything they have in inflation-adjusted terms as legacies — this is simply not practicable for most. There are too many variables to plan any of these wishes to perfection, but you could decide to draw more or less according to what you want to leave. Moreover, quite a lot of people like the idea of giving significant gifts to children and grandchildren in their own lifetimes. This is kind of an early inheritance given while you are still alive to enjoy the act of giving and see the difference it makes. Such early gifts will also affect the amount of capital you have to draw down on. These gifts need to be allowed for to some extent and could lead to alterations in your retirement plans.
- **Inheritance — receiving.** I am very cautious when people start to talk about inheritances they are likely to receive. I do not like to factor them into a plan until they are actually received (never count your money until it is in the tin) because I have often seen expected inheritances either turn out to be a lot less than expected or to not materialise at all. This can be for a range of reasons: perhaps the deceased did not have as much as everyone thought, or there was a problem with a big asset (like the house), or the family fell out with each other, etc. Perhaps I am too conservative about this, but I do not like treating inheritances that are likely to come one day as if they will definitely be received. Having said that, with the price of houses as they are, some people do receive major inheritances even when the deceased owned a house and little more. This can be life-changing for the recipient and gives a most welcome boost to retirement plans.

- **Expenditure.** This is the most obvious factor of them all to adjust — the problem is that if you cannot make the numbers work and have to reduce expenditure, you are probably reducing your potential lifestyle. To some extent this cuts across the aim of the process which is to have a quality retirement. Nevertheless, as I show in chapter 2, expenditure levels in retirement can (and probably will) vary — at different times they will be higher than other times. Moreover, it is worth doing a budget and then repeatedly going over that budget. This process will mean thinking about what is important to you and what is not so important — for example, you may decide that the flexibility of having two cars in retirement is not as important as an annual ski holiday. This is not about being mean and scrimping — it is about being very clear on your priorities.
- Time in retirement. Unfortunately, we cannot adjust our age to make the numbers fit. However, we can choose when we are going to retire and, by delaying retirement, we can choose how many years the money has to last. This delay gives several financial advantages (although continuing to work may not be what you want from a lifestyle point of view), including the obvious one that your money does not have to last as long (see below).

Delaying retirement

Putting off retirement may be a reasonable option for some people — but not for others. Those who want (or need) to retire whatever the numbers will quite possibly just have to make some compromises. Perhaps you will have to forgo buying the camper van (and rent one instead when you want one) or downsize the house even more than you thought. However, compromise may not fit with the kind of retirement that you have imagined — in which case continuing to work may be the only option.

A 2018 study by BNZ found that 46% of Kiwis wanted to keep working beyond age 65. Most of these people wanted to carry on working part-time with a smaller number wanting to work full-time. There was a range of reasons for wanting to continue to work: work brings them satisfaction, the chance to use their abilities and skills, and social contact.

However, 31% of those surveyed said they would have to work because they need the money (perhaps they need to pay off a loan or increase savings or simply could not imagine living on NZ Super alone). These are the people who have tried to do a plan to retire but could not make the numbers work.

Delaying retirement and continuing to work for a few years will help your situation and, when you do actually retire, you ought to be in a better position financially. This is because:

1. Your extra income should mean you have more savings (or, perhaps, no debt). You should remember that after age 65 the Government will not contribute to KiwiSaver. Employers do not have to contribute to over 65s' KiwiSavers (which is a disgrace in my view — I cannot see why workers should lose 3% of their incomes on their 65th birthday). Of course, you can carry on contributing to KiwiSaver and if you are hoping to grow your savings, you should certainly do so (and it is possible that your employer may carry on contributing even though they are not obliged to do so).

2. With no drawings coming from your KiwiSaver or other investments, your savings will grow even without contributions (and they will probably have the addition of NZ Super which you should receive from age 65). Your retirement savings will continue to earn returns and these will compound until such time as you retire and start to draw on them for income in retirement. Even if you work part-time from age 65, your savings should still grow.

3. The money needs to last a shorter time. If you work for (say) five years after you turn 65, you should be able to adopt a

higher drawdown rate. Remember that under the 4% rule your money ought to last 30 years — which would take you to 95 years. However, if you worked for five years (until age 70) you have five years less drawing — i.e. you would draw for 25 years to get to the same age. This could mean that you could draw 5% or 6% (instead of 4%) from the portfolio.

Example — The effect of part-time work post retirement

To see how these three benefits of delay may help, let's look at Lucy who at age 65 has a mortgage-free house and $400,000 of investments. At a 4% drawdown rate, she would have $16,0000 per annum (in addition to NZ Super) to fund her lifestyle, and she believes this to be insufficient.

However, let's say that Lucy moves from working full-time to 3.5 days per week, and commits to keep working at that level for another five years, until age 70. At that level of work, Lucy can no longer continue to save, although she can continue to contribute to her KiwiSaver. While the government will no longer contribute, her employers might agree to continue to match her 3% of savings.

Lucy calculates that her savings (including KiwiSaver) will have grown to $460,000. On retirement, she can apply a higher drawdown rate: because she will have less time in retirement relying on savings, instead of drawing 4%, she decides to go for broke, have a ball, and draw 6% p.a. This means instead of having $16,000 p.a. to supplement NZ Super, she has $27,600 p.a.

Summary

	Age 65	Age 70
Savings	$400,000	$460,000
Drawdown rate	4%	6%
Income from investments	$16,000p.a.	$27,600 p.a.

So, waiting a bit longer to retire certainly has benefits from a financial point of view. Of course, you will be that much older, and you will have missed some of your best years. There will also be many who just want to leave work and retire as soon as they can.

Ultimately, you will have to ask whether you have enough to fund the lifestyle that you want. Will you have to rethink how you live, or even where you live? Perhaps you will have to postpone retirement and work a few more years.

When the reality of retirement is close, there is a multitude of things to think about, and, often enough, agree with a partner. This multitude is not only about money, finance and investment — there are also questions of where you will live, what 'toys' you might buy pre-retirement, travel, what does a typical day look like, will you do any work, and where, when and how you will see friends and family.

Crucially, all the plans and sub-plans need to fit together. It is this which makes retirement planning an iterative process. Each decision can impact other decisions: for example, if you decide to move to Nelson, it has ramifications for how much money you will have, and, of course, on relationships with family and friends. Moving to Nelson could impact your budget (more money may be spent on travel to see family and friends) and it could impact on the 'toys' that you have (could you live in Nelson without having a boat?).

So, you have to work around and around the issues until they are all agreed and fit together. This ought to be done well before retirement — planning shows you how much you are going to need which allows you to set goals to work towards. Your retirement plans are unlikely to work perfectly but the chances are if you plan for your best retirement, that is what you will get.

I reckon #2 — Retirement is about more than the money stuff
Planning retirement is not an easy matter. This book largely looks at the financial issues, but, while there is plenty to decide on how to make the money work, there are many lifestyle issues too. As you approach or move into retirement, there is a sense of urgency about doing things before it is too late.

Relationships can come under pressure. I have never seen figures on this, but it does appear that retirement sees more relationships fail (there are enough of these for a new term to be coined — silver splitters — implying that a split is common enough).

Retirement is a major development stage, which comes at a time when we are not so good at change. Couples, long separated by work and other activities, are suddenly thrown together: she never thought that she would have him lying on the couch watching cricket all day, and he never realised how much time she spent at golf. Little wonder that with such change, many people put their toes in the retirement water only to pull them out again.

CHAPTER 2
Spending in Retirement

There is an old financial planning rule of thumb that says in retirement your spending will be approximately 75% of what it was before retirement. The thinking behind this is that on retirement your expenditure falls because you no longer commute, no longer need work clothes, perhaps you sell one car, eat out (or have takeaways) less often. A range of costs drop out and so you spend less.

If only it were that simple!

In fact, in my experience, rather than costs falling on retirement, sometimes they actually rise — you have time to shop, time to travel, time to do sports, gardening and other activities, and these things cost. The kinds of retirement that many people now imagine require more money than rushing off to work every day.

Studies confirm my own narrow experience of client behaviour when they hit retirement: spending in retirement is not a straight line; you will not have a consistent rate of expenditure from the time you pick up the gold watch at age 65 through to when you die 20 or 30 years later. Just as it does throughout your working life, your lifestyle and expenditure changes.

Many studies show that on retirement expenditure does drop

a little — and then continues to gradually reduce. That is across a population, but within that whole group of retirees there is a great deal of variation, and in my experience, there are a lot of people whose expenditure actually rises on retirement, while for others (perhaps the majority) it falls a little. And then, of course, there will be people whose expenditure falls a lot. Within those averages there are a lot of unders and overs.

Crucially, your retirement is your retirement; and your expenditure will be your expenditure. It is interesting, maybe even useful, to know the averages, but you cannot rely on them.

You need to think about your own expenditure and do some numbers. Your expenditure may be nothing like average: it may be higher at different times; it may be spent on different things. Rules of thumb are always just that: they deal with the average, they do not deal with you. Like your drawdown rate (see chapter 4), you need to personalise this as far as you can.

The three stages of retirement

Retirement is a long time of life and within it are several stages. Most retirement experts divide retirement into three stages which are sometimes called:

1. All go (aged 65 to 74)
2. Slow go (aged 75 to 84)
3. No go (aged 85 onwards)

These stages are not set in stone, and you should not bother setting your watch by them. There are plenty of people who are still racing around running their businesses, sailing their yacht, coaching sport or open water swimming well into their eighties.

However, although they deal with averages, setting these stages is quite useful because there are lifestyle (and financial) issues which impact on each. And, although the timing may not match everyone's experience, they are the stages that most of us will go

Retirement spending

• Spending during retirement fluctuates through three phases.

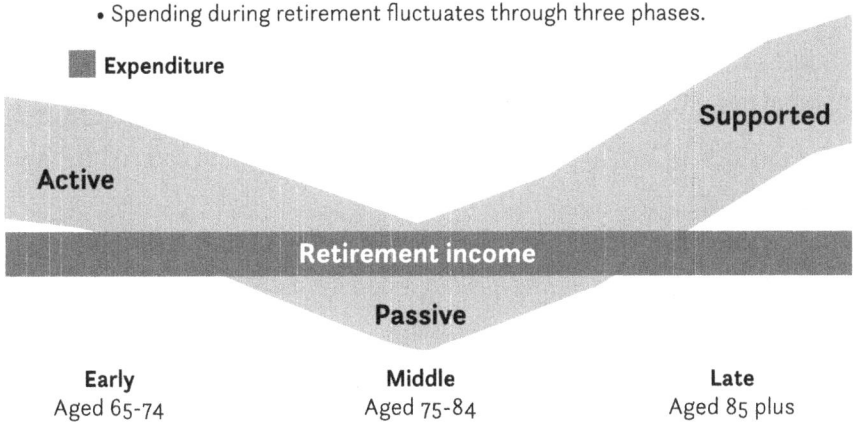

Source: Commission for Financial Capability

throughout our retirements. They also show that even with the outliers, the people who hit a stage either long before or long after most others, largely there is a pattern of slowing down.

Matching drawdown to retirement stage

This slowing down has important financial implications and matching your drawdown to expenditure is important — expenditure will fall as you move through retirement, and so your income can fall as well.

As the graph above shows, it is likely that most people will spend more money in the 'all go' stage than they will in the two later stages. Having said this, for some, the 'no go' stage can also be expensive if there is a lot of health care expense required and this needs to be funded out of your own pocket rather than through the public system, health insurance or through family. (In some countries, the 'no go' stage is shown as a costly time which probably tells us something about their health systems.)

Perhaps most importantly, you should put aside the idea of

a single amount of unvarying income throughout your entire retirement. The idea that in retirement you will spend 75% of the amount you did before retirement may possibly be true over the entirety of retirement, but this seems to me to be most unlikely to be a flat line throughout. There will be periods of high expenditure and periods of low expenditure and these need to be catered for and planned for.

For this reason, the 4% rule (see chapter 4) is only useful as a guide: you will not want or need a constant amount of income through all those years of retirement.

Underspending

Most people imagine they will spend all of their savings during retirement and leave other things (e.g. the house) as inheritance. If this is the aim, many fail. Rather than fail because they have overspent and end up impoverished, they underspend and finish their lives with a lot of capital left. This is understandable: it is hard to set a retirement spending plan in place and execute that plan perfectly to go out on the last dollar — there are just too many uncertainties for that. Nevertheless, the chances are you can spend more than you think. This should not be wasteful (i.e. you spend money simply because you can) but if there are things and experiences that will bring happiness and satisfaction, that should be what retirement and your retirement savings are for.

All go

For some people, living in the 'All go' stage of retirement is more expensive than when they were still working. These people are mostly well off and they travel, refurbish their homes, update cars regularly and generally have the best things. They may have been hectic and busy throughout their working lives but in retirement they have time to spend. They enjoy spending money and now that they are not busy working, they can afford to do so.

For people of more modest means, expenditure is likely to reduce. Most people are instinctively cautious and concerned that the money will not last their whole lives. We fear running out of money more than just about anything else — the risk that the money will run out is a bigger concern than the prospect that we won't spend enough to have a better lifestyle. We would rather be safe than sorry.

People are, therefore, careful, knowing that retirement stretches out before them for two or three decades and that anything might happen in that time. They also have no experience of living off a portfolio — they are venturing into the unknown, perhaps with little or no idea of what returns they should expect or what a reasonable drawdown rate ought to be.

Moreover, you should have no illusions regarding the discomfort you will feel as your savings reduce. If you are like most people and spending capital as well as investments returns, you will watch the amount of your investments gradually fall.

There are many uncertainties when using an investment portfolio in retirement and many people instinctively retreat to safety. The unknowns in embarking on a whole new time of life make a cautious approach understandable, and caution leads directly to underspending.

It is in the first stage that this underspend happens. It may not become apparent or obvious until much later, but it is the drawdown rate that you choose at the start of retirement that sets the tone for all of retirement Obviously, you cannot spend whatever you like at the start — you do need to think about the future — but to some degree you have to put aside those things that are making you overcautious and overcareful.

That is why I often recommend a drawdown of 6% of the initial portfolio instead of the much safer 4%. This makes quite a difference: if you had $500,000, a drawdown of 4% would allow you $20,000 p.a., whereas a drawdown of 6% gives $30,000 p.a. That extra $10,000 p.a. of income is significant — it is an extra $200 per week which lets you do quite a lot more things at a time which is really a last chance to do and have some things.

Slow go

Life and expenditure diminish during the 'Slow go' period, sometimes slowly and sometimes in quite big jumps. People can be aware that they will spend less and so it can suddenly move lower; other times lower expenditure happens in a very gradual, unnoticeable way.

My mother was an enthusiastic traveller and, in retirement, tried to get away overseas most years. Once, in her late seventies, she came back from several weeks in Italy, and delighted to be home, dropped into her favourite chair and said very quietly, 'I think that'll be my last trip.' It was — I don't think she ever left Christchurch again (let alone New Zealand) and she lived another two decades with her memories of travel all over the world.

That is an example of a quite sudden change: had my mother lived to a budget, that decision and announcement would have meant that she could have taken $10,000 out of the expenditure line each year.

Other changes creep up on you during the 'Slow go' period. A slow reduction in expenditures on food and drink, the car used only to go to the supermarket with fewer (or no) trips out of town, gradually eating out less (it's too noisy). None of these things require a sudden and dramatic reduction in the budget, they happen slowly without anyone taking much notice.

These two things — the slow, small and gradual, and the big and dramatic — are quite different. The big things can be planned for — you can make an estimate of when you might move to only having one car, or when you will stop travelling. The smaller things that you stop doing (no longer playing some sports, doing less in the garden) are usually small ticket items by comparison and do not suddenly stop. Nevertheless, these changes will happen and can be planned — for example, starting at age 75, you might plan to reduce expenditure each year by 2%.

None of these adjustments are fool proof or likely to be perfectly accurate. However, it is valid for you to start to reduce expenditure from a certain age and, with this expenditure reduction, plan to draw correspondingly less from your portfolio.

The name 'slow go' has always seemed to me to be an unkind description of this stage. Certainly, you will become less active, and, for many people, the activity may shift from doing physical stuff to other less physical things. People do not talk much about this shift from having an external focus to a more internal life but there is plenty of literature that supports it.

In any event, most people can plan to spend less at this stage as activities fall by the wayside. Sometimes this just seems to happen naturally, almost without people knowing it; but whenever it happens, it will happen. Most people would say that the 'slow go' starts at about age 75 and as an average that seems about right. However, like a lot of retirement planning there is a great deal of variability and while 75 is a good marker for planned expenditure to start to fall, there will be plenty who will be at this stage sooner or later than that.

No go

'No go' is an even more unkind description for a stage of retirement. It is also inaccurate in many cases because there are plenty of people in their late-eighties and early-nineties who are still quite active and enjoying life. After all, if you have got to age 65, life expectancy figures suggest that you will last a good while yet (for a 65-year-old woman, life expectancy is 90 years and for a man it is 87 years). Within those averages there are again unders and overs with many people exceeding those numbers and still living well at about the time they should be expecting to be in fairly sharp decline.

However, although many people are sprightly and in possession of all their faculties at this age, this is not a book about health but one about finances. And it is a common observation (backed by studies) that expenditure has fallen by the time you reach eighty and, almost certainly, by ninety.

It seems to me that it is reasonable to plan for a fall in expenditure at this time of life; late in life, you are unlikely to be spending anything like what you used to spend.

The exception to this could be health and personal care expenses (see below). These expenses will continue to rise, particularly for people who have maintained their health insurance and for others who have decided to receive most of their healthcare through the private system. It may also rise for people who choose to retain their independence and buy in extra services to enable this to happen.

Healthcare expenditure

As I write, I have seen several friends and family members struggle to access the public health system. I have heard multiple stories of people spending hours in the emergency department of hospitals, and of situations where overworked nurses say they will be back in a few minutes but are never seen again.

While I am drawing from a relatively small data set, it seems to me that although the people working in the public health system are excellent, the system is broken and lacks funding for what it is expected to do. I watch what is happening and have decided to avoid the public health system as far as I can.

It seems to me that in terms of our health expenditure in retirement we have three choices:

1. Commit to the private system and pay insurance;
2. Commit to the private system and self-insure (i.e. be ready to pay for your own treatment); or
3. Commit to the public system and hope.

If you look at these options, there are two main decisions:

1. Can you afford the private system? This is not an easy question, because you have to take a guess at the amount of healthcare you will need and how much of that you will want done quickly in the private system. These are unknowns and, although most people would probably always prefer to go private, whether you can afford to is mostly going to be a matter of judgment after considering your financial position and your health.
2. If you decide you want to go private, how will you fund this? The choices are insurance and self-funding (self-insurance). A part of this decision will be based on the likelihood of you making claims on your health insurance. This is simply another way of asking whether your health is likely to be better or worse than average as you move through retirement and into old age. Again, there are many unknowns, and you will have to make an assessment. Remember, of course, that although health insurance will seem eye-wateringly expensive as you become older, it simply reflects the average payouts that the insurance will have to make — the insurance company sets its premiums according to claims plus some extra to meet its costs and make a profit. Your actual healthcare costs may be greater or less than your insurance costs. Paying the insurance company an amount to let it make a profit is simply the price you pay to rid yourself of the risk that you will have to pay more than average if you self-insure.

Budgetting for the 3 stages of retirement

The word 'budget' gets a very bad rap — it has connotations of scrimping and saving and living on as little as you possibly can.

In fact, 'budget' just means a plan for your income and expenditure; this chapter and the preceding one have been about exactly that: will you have enough income to meet your desired expenditure throughout retirement?

To complete the plan, you will need to imagine your future life in retirement and put a cost on it. You should probably start by trying to imagine a typical day, a typical week, a typical month, and a typical year. A good place to start is buying one of those wall charts (or the electronic equivalent) which take the form of a big calendar. You can fill this in with the kind of activities you will be doing: travel, visiting family, sports, entertainment, etc.

If you know how often you will travel and where, you can put a cost on it; if you know how much you will ski, you can put a cost on it. This process may give you an amount for your expenditure in the first stage of retirement, but that number then has to pass a sniff test, i.e. does that number seem about right?

Most people have some idea of the amount of money that they have been spending; does the number that you have come up with for the start of retirement feel about right? If not, check whether it is too high or too low, go back and have another look.

At the same time as you are doing this it would be a good idea to have a look at a budget calculator — www.sorted.org.nz is probably the best. This is not because it adds up the expenditure figures any better than any other, but because it captures all the main expenditure categories and ensures that nothing is missed.

It is reasonable for you to be able to imagine your expenditure in the first 'All go' stage of retirement but imagining the latter two stages are likely to be much harder. Whereas the 'All go' stage is to some extent a continuation of your current life, we have no experience of these latter two stages. However, these two are a big part of retirement and you need to have a plan to fund them.

For planning purposes, it seems reasonable to me that you reduce planned expenditure by 20% at age 75, and then by another 10% at age 85. These reductions are more than a bit approximate, but I doubt that you will get much closer to accurate figures by trying to pinpoint your expenditures.

Setting aside money for each expenditure category

There is another way to look at your incomes and expenditures plans in retirement. It does not save you from the budgeting but falls back on using the old 'jam jar' approach to managing money.

The jam jar approach was to have a jar for each category of spending. My grandmother used this: she had a jar for milk and bread, a jar for rent, a jar for groceries, etc. When she got her weekly income, she dropped the required number of shillings in each jar so that she could be sure that she would have enough money to pay rent, buy milk and bread, etc. (In those days, there were no credit cards so you had to make sure you had enough, or rent would go unpaid, and that meant trouble.)

For retirement in the 2020s, the jam jar approach means that you have funds or other sets of investments for each of your major expenditure categories. You may decide that you have four main areas of expenditure:
- housing
- health
- groceries, entertainment
- activities, travel, hobbies, transport

Each of these four categories could be covered by an investment fund or other stream of income that can be used to draw down to meet those types of expenses.

Example: The Jam Jar approach to categorising expenses

I can illustrate this best by using the example of Ruth. Ruth had a mortgage-free house and investments of $500,000. She had four different potential income streams:

1. NZ Super $20,000 p.a. This was used to pay her groceries and entertainment costs.

2. A KiwiSaver fund with $50,000. This was set aside to pay for her healthcare.
3. A drawdown fund of $100,000. Ruth planned to withdraw $4,500 p.a. which would cover rates.
4. A balanced fund of $350,000 invested by her financial adviser from which she planned a drawdown of 6% p.a. This would give her $21,000 each year which would cover transport, travel and activities.

All up, Ruth has total income of $47,500 p.a. (plus, her funds for healthcare). She has divided her income into these streams so she knows from where she is going to draw funds. She also knows that some of her expense items will decline over the years; she is not sure when this will happen but knows it will.

There are risks in this approach, of course. Maybe $50,000 would prove to be insufficient for her healthcare, or perhaps her balanced fund with the financial advisers would have a few years of poor investment performance. However, with any retirement plan, you have to acknowledge that there are uncertainties and risks. There is nothing in the future about which you can be 100% certain, but Ruth can be fairly sure that the drawings on her balanced fund with the financial advisers (which pays for things like activities and travel) will reduce over time.

Your plan is **your** plan

As we will discuss further in chapter 4, rules of thumb like the 4% rule are not personalised for your circumstances. They are designed to give you a flat, constant income through the decades of retirement, but which are unlikely to meet your needs.

There is a very strong case for personalising not just your expected income but also your expenditure. Rules of thumb like the 4% rule for your drawdown or the 75% rule for expenditure are useful as an indication of what we can expect but reflect averages, at best, with no account of your personal situation.

Many people have their own spreadsheet for income and expenditure in retirement — sometimes they have done these spreadsheets themselves or have had a financial adviser prepare it for them. Who does the spreadsheet is neither here nor there — it is the assumptions that go into the spreadsheet that are the tricky part. The whole point of doing the spreadsheet is to personalise some of these assumptions. However, I have seen many spreadsheets based on assumptions that seem to me to be quite unlikely, and I think they would prove to be wrong.

When preparing your spreadsheet, these are the most important assumptions you will have to make:

- **Investment returns:** Assume that you invest in a balanced fund, the returns from this are likely to be around 5% p.a. but you have to remember that this figure is before tax and fees. Tax and fees will be personal to you and you will need to deduct them from the 5% p.a. For most people, the net return (after tax and fees) could be approximately 3.5% p.a.
- **Inflation:** You need to make an estimate regarding inflation as this will affect both your spending costs and your income from investment returns. The best figure for inflation over the long term is usually the mid-point of the Reserve Bank's inflation target. This target is 1–3% and the mid-point of this is 2%.
- **Life expectancy:** The average life expectancy for a 65-year-old is approximately 90 years for a woman and 87 years for a man. To make assumptions for your spreadsheet, you will need to try to estimate when you want your money to run out (most people would say a couple of years after they expect to die to give themselves a little leeway). However, knowing when you will die is something that few of us know (fortunately, probably) particularly as we guess from a decade or decades out. Parental or family longevity along with an assessment of your own health may give an indication, but there is no good

way to estimate life expectancy accurately, so an approximation will need to do.

Drawdown

Your drawdown will need to match the gap between NZ Super and your total expenditure. If it does not adequately fill that gap, you need to rethink your plans. You will have to make assumptions regarding the drawdown rate at the start of retirement (perhaps 6%) and commit to decrease your drawdown rate as you get older and plan to spend less. This may need some adjustment as you try to make the numbers work (see chapter 4).

Sequencing of returns

You cannot make any assumptions on the sequencing of investment returns. Even the very best crystal ball cannot tell us whether we will have strong returns at the start of retirement and poor returns towards the end, or vice versa. There is simply no way of assessing this and, therefore, you will need to assume that returns will be consistent and constant throughout retirement.

In reality, investment returns will be anything but constant or consistent: history tells us they will be volatile. The sequencing of returns remains the biggest risk that retirees face and holding some cash is the best way of mitigating it (see page 64).

Personalise — where you can

A personalised plan, set out on a spreadsheet with reasonable assumptions is a very good way of going into retirement. Although it will not be perfectly accurate, it ought to give comfort and, as you go through retirement, the spreadsheet can be revisited to see where things are going adrift. Changes can then be made early enough to try to bring the plan back into line and so saving further heartbreak down the track. When you have worked out your likely expenditures through retirement, you can try to match them with income. The remaining chapters in this section of the book are about the income side of the plan — but, before you start to worry about how much income you will have, you need a fairly clear view of what your expenditures will be.

> **I reckon #3 — That old 'should I keep my health insurance' chestnut**
> In my advisory practice, health insurance — whether to have it or not — is the one thing I could depend on as being a topic for discussion. As people traverse their fifties and sixties, the amount that you pay becomes steeper and steeper until, in your seventies, it becomes a near vertical cliff. That prompts a discussion.
> My take on this has been:
> 1. The public system will treat (and treat well) major conditions that need care urgently.
> 2. Insurance is always about covering risk that you cannot afford to take. That might mean insuring major surgery that could be slow in the public system (e.g. joint replacement).
> 3. On average most insurance does not have exceptionally high margins and, therefore, the amount you pay is about what the average person would spend.
>
> Given what I perceive to be the parlous state of the public system (I would love to be shown wrong on this), I do think that you should be ready to pay for some private care if possible. Therefore, I reckon that Ruth (in the example on page 53) has got things about right. I have:
> 1. Some health insurance with a high excess and which covers surgery only; and
> 2. A fund for covering medical care, diagnostics, etc. (in my case I have my KiwiSaver fund).

CHAPTER 3
Making your Money Last as Long as you do

For many years, people in retirement held their savings in bank deposits or similar fixed interest securities. The interest would be received (perhaps monthly, or perhaps six-monthly) and spent. On maturity, the investment would be rolled over into a new similar investment. This process was repeated and the continual rolling over of interest-earning securities and bank deposits was probably the main drawdown strategy for most retirees.

This strategy seemed to work reasonably well. Interest rates were higher than they are now, and the income received from interest payments was enough. Importantly, life expectancy was lower and people were probably less active than they are today and had fewer expenditure demands placed on them in retirement.

However, the higher interest rates were probably really an illusion at most times. Certainly, headline rates were higher (often much higher), but so too was income tax and inflation. Therefore, real interest rates (after inflation and tax) were often very low, even negative. People following this strategy were losing spending power each year and there was a great deal of talk about it all being very tough for people on 'fixed incomes' (a code for retired people).

In reality, although the rolling over of interest-bearing securities seemed to work, lower life expectancy masked the fact that it was not a good strategy. Quite simply, a lot of people died before inflation had a chance to wreck their retirement plans. In 1950, the retirement age was 60 years, meaning that on average people only enjoyed nine years of retirement. Today, with retirement age at 65, people on average have 17 years in retirement.

Therefore, today people must fund an additional eight years of retirement and low returns from interest-bearing investments no longer work, if they ever did. Term deposits no longer cut the mustard.

At the same time, two other things have happened:
1. People have become more willing to spend capital; and
2. It is much easier to access financial markets which give higher returns.

There are still a good number of people who continue to be wedded to bank deposits and fixed interest investments. Such people think that these kinds of investments are safer, even though by taking out a term deposit you are almost certain to lose money in real terms. In my lifetime, there has been a swing towards diversified portfolios, and, although not everybody is quite there yet, things are improving.

Retirement income — the new way

While a few people still adopt the term deposit strategy, a much smarter plan is to have a diversified fund and draw a defined amount from this each fortnight. This diversified fund or portfolio could be a managed fund or funds (possibly a KiwiSaver account), a fund put together by a financial adviser, or, less commonly, a set of investments you directly manage yourself. A diversified fund will give exposure to all asset classes and be diversified within all asset classes.

At the moment, you cannot expect this diversified portfolio to spin off much cash income — interest rates are low, and so too are dividend yields. In the past, people may have lived happily enough on the interest and/or dividends they received but that is no longer the case. The idea of investing for income to live on is gone.

Instead, you will draw from the portfolio a set amount regardless of the cash returns that the portfolio or fund is returning. The fund will certainly make returns, but these will be made up of interest, dividends and capital gains.

These returns will accrue to the fund; however, it is quite likely that you will draw more than these total returns — and that means you will effectively be withdrawing a part of the capital, i.e. you will be running the fund down.

It is necessary for you to draw a pre-determined and constant amount because that is what you will be living on. You will draw on the fund every fortnight (or month) and that amount needs to be set at a level which will run the fund down — but not too quickly or too slowly. Over long periods of time the amount that you draw may change, however, over short periods of time (fortnightly or monthly), it will remain consistent as you draw down to pay bills.

It's important to remember that you will not be living solely on the income or gains that the fund earns. The fund will have investment returns but almost regardless of what they are, you will draw down an amount that you have set at the beginning.

It is difficult to set a sustainable drawdown rate, and this chapter, along with the next, aims to help you set your rate of drawdown. Rest assured that investment returns are calculated into setting drawdown rates but the idea of living solely on those returns is gone.

Spending capital

Whatever the drawdown rate you choose, unless it is very low it is most likely to include your investment returns and, each year, a little bit of your original capital as well.

Throughout retirement you will make constant withdrawals —

possibly following the 4% rule or some other rule of thumb. At the beginning of retirement, you will spend mostly investment returns and only a little of your investment capital. However, as time goes on and your capital gradually reduces, you have smaller investment returns (because you have less capital to generate returns) and so a greater proportion of your withdrawals from the portfolio is made up of capital.

You may be drawing a standard $1,000 per fortnight from your investments but if you track the amount that you have in your investments, you will notice it reducing — slowly at first, faster towards the end. Graphically the amount that you have in your investment fund will look like this:

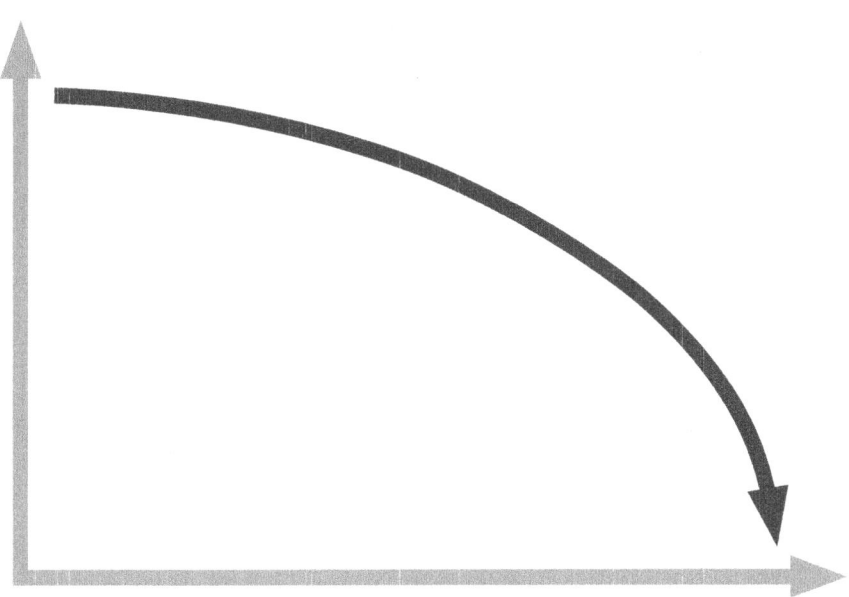

There is good way to think of this: imagine a couple who spend their whole lives as chicken farmers. They buy a dozen chickens (their capital) and, when they lay, they sell their eggs (their investment returns). However, they realise that selling a dozen or so eggs is not going to make them rich, and so, instead of selling all of their eggs, they hold one back each day (i.e. they save it). They keep this egg until it hatches, and this grows their flock. Saving that egg grows their capital and they end up with a magnificent flock of chickens, which lay plenty of eggs.

Come retirement, our farmers stop selling their eggs and instead start to consume them — eggs for breakfast, lunch and dinner (boring, perhaps, but nutritious enough). However, their eggs do not go quite far enough (they are not quite rich enough, there are not quite enough chickens laying) and so they have to supplement their diet of eggs by killing the odd chicken. Roast chicken makes a welcome relief from all those eggs, but as chickens are killed and eaten, there are fewer to lay for them — and so the number of eggs available to eat reduces. Gradually, the couple's diet changes: they find that they are eating fewer eggs (income) and more chickens (capital). The race is on to see if they will have enough for their whole retirement — if they can get the timing just right, there will be no chickens to trade with the undertaker for decent funerals.

In the chicken farming example, there is a clear distinction between eggs and chickens, income and capital. In real life with a diversified portfolio, you will simply draw the same $1,000 each fortnight. Certainly, you will be able to figure out what your investment returns are, and you will be able to keep track of the amount of capital you have, but each fortnight, you will draw $1,000 regardless (or, nearly regardless — if the markets are in a serious downturn, you may stop or reduce drawings for a bit if you can).

The key for you is to decide how much you can draw down and still pay the undertaker. The chicken farmers had the same problem — they could have been gluttons or starved themselves. I could offer them no advice on this — I do not know the reproduction rate for chickens, nor have any idea the number of eggs or chickens you need to eat and have a good life.

Fortunately, when it comes to money, I am not so blind. This is because many people have the same drawdown problem, and we now have some rules of thumb to work from. These give the rate of drawdown which should be safe for you. They are not perfect because over the course of a long retirement anything might happen. They are, nevertheless, a good starting point and, even though you may need to make adjustments during retirement, they ought to give a fairly reasonable idea of how much to draw down each year.

One big problem — volatility

The problem with asking people to adopt a retirement portfolio with exposures to shares, listed property and a range of fixed interest securities, and asking them to draw regularly through thick and thin, is that we all know such a portfolio will be volatile. Retirees are looking for steady income — they need it to buy the groceries and pay their utility bills every week or every month. And this diversified portfolio will not give steady returns — it will be subject to all of the vagaries of financial markets.

There is, therefore, a mismatch between your investment goals (steady income) and a diversified portfolio with its exposures to shares and listed property and subsequent volatility.

However, you cannot simply revert to using term deposits — at the moment (and, quite probably at most times) the only thing steady about bank deposits and fixed interest investments is the loss that you incur. If you took out a term deposit, it will be near certain to make you poorer in real terms; fixed interest investments will give even more losses if interest rates rise, and you are stuck on that rate for some years. In no other investment area that I know of do people knowingly go into an investment that is sure to lose!

It may seem unfortunate, but volatility from a diversified portfolio is inevitable — you will have to take on that risk. However, market risk can be mitigated, and it is entirely possible to set up your finances so you can make steady drawings. Although volatility can be mitigated, it cannot be completely abolished — you must take a risk to get a return.

A solution to volatility risk: A lake of cash

The best way to mitigate the risk of this volatility is to be sure to hold some ready cash in the bank outside the portfolio. The purpose of this cash is that when markets are down you can live off the cash for a year or two.

Each time you draw down on the portfolio, you will effectively be selling a small amount of your investments (remember that in drawing down, you are not simply taking the returns but also an amount of your capital). If markets are down and, as you must to be able to live, you continue to draw from the fund, you are effectively selling at a time when values are low — this is not what you want to do as an investor and holding some cash on the side means you can avoid selling at least for a time.

An amount of cash outside your investment portfolio acts as a buffer against periods of poor returns. This cash (probably set up in term deposits with varying maturities) is there to use when things get bad and you would prefer not to draw on the portfolio because it has fallen in value.

I generally say that you should hold an amount of cash sufficient to get you through two years without touching the investment portfolio. That would mean that the couple who have $500,000 and who are following the 4% rule would expect to draw $20,000 each year. To give them a buffer of two years, they would need to have $40,000 outside the portfolio. This may mean that they only invest $460,000 in the portfolio at the start.

A further step in holding cash is to increase or decrease the amount depending on whether times are good or bad. During times of poor returns, you will almost certainly reduce the amount of cash that you have as you draw on it to live. This after all is the whole purpose of having it.

However, you may think to increase the amount that you have when times are good, and returns are much higher than you would expect. Putting aside some of these super-returns will increase your buffer against bad times and so, if a recession or market downturn goes on for a long time, you may be able to continue to get through without selling any part of the portfolio.

Intuitively, this squirrel-like approach works for a lot of people. Putting aside even greater reserves of nuts against an especially hard and long winter is what most of today's retirees had banged into them at school or by parents. Putting excess returns away during summer for those cold, rainy days of winter is what a lot of us were brought up with.

Holding these amounts of cash will reduce investment returns. However, having the ability to sit out a crash without drawing on an investment portfolio and, therefore, avoid having to sell during the worst of the crash is worth that loss of return.

In my experience, people going into retirement like the idea of holding this lake of cash. It gives them a feeling of security to know that there is two years of living regardless of what may happen to their portfolio.

Sequencing risk

This is a risk that we all face as we invest in retirement regardless of our drawdown rate. The risk is that the timing of bad investment returns happens to be bad for you. We all know that at times there will be good returns but at other times they will not be good. When these good and bad returns come, i.e. the sequence of returns, is important.

For instance, at the start of retirement, you have the most money invested because you have not yet drawn down much capital. If there is a major market slump at the start, your losses will be greater in dollar terms and most people will be drawing down a larger amount of capital to fund their more expensive lifestyles. If there was a major slump towards the end of your retirement, it would matter less — there is less money for the slump to take and, in any event, you are likely to be drawing less.

We know that even a balanced fund will be volatile. Shares and property, in particular, will go up and down in value and take the total value of your savings with it. We also know that periodically there are major market meltdowns. I have lived and invested through four of these (the 1987 crash, the dot-com crash, the global financial crisis and COVID-19). None was pleasant (although buying cheap shares during them was good in some cases). However, when these struck, I was in work and had income — I was not dependent on my portfolio for investment returns.

These sorts of crashes are much harder on the retired. They see the source of their income — their very living — disappear. This is exacerbated by the financial commentariat who, in full force, shout about the demise of the world and civilisation as we know it. The noise of the markets is just as frightening as the crash itself. You can be sure that there will be someone saying things which give investors no hope for the future.

Commentariat aside, you can expect financial market crashes during the 20 or 30 years of your retirement. The problem for retired people is that they are still drawing on their investments and, because investment returns during a crash are poor, they are drawing capital.

Drawing capital means selling shares and other investments — and during a crash, the very time when markets are down, is not a time to be selling.

To take an extreme example, if you put your $500,000 life savings into a fund and the next day the fund value fell by 20%, you would now only have $400,000 to draw from. We can expect markets to bounce back eventually but, in the meantime, you are effectively selling down during a time of investment woe — you are selling cheap.

Each withdrawal that you make takes a bite out of the balance and means that money is not there any longer to help when the inevitable recovery comes.

Dollar-cost averaging

You should establish your retirement portfolio or fund early (ideally when you are still working) and build it by dollar cost averaging. Dollar-cost averaging means drip feeding your money into the fund regularly over a year or two instead of dropping the whole lot in on just one day. If you have sold the farm and put all the money into a fund on day one, that may prove to be a very good day (the markets have fallen a lot) or it may prove to be a very bad day (the markets collapse on the day after you deposit your money).

Dollar-cost averaging means that every month or quarter you put money into the fund regardless of whether the markets are up or down. This means that some of your payments will go into the markets on good days and some on bad days but, over the year or two that you drip feed into the markets, you will be investing at an average value.

For example, you sell your business for $500,000 and agree that you will continue to work in the business for two years before you retire. You identify an adviser who will manage the money for you and set up a retirement account. You agree with your advisor that you will dollar-cost average into the investment over one year. This means that you will make 12 monthly payments into the account over one year. The exact maths would say that each of these 12 payments would be $41,666, but to make things simple, I would probably simply transfer $40,000 each time and make up for the difference by making contributions for another month.

Some advisers do not like dollar-cost averaging. From their point of view, they see it as requiring a bit more work and, of course, they get paid according to how much of your money they are managing, so are incentivised to get the money in and invested as soon as they can. You may have to stand up to them and insist!

Of course, dollar-cost averaging does not help if the sequence of returns was such that the major fall happened the day after you have completed the portfolio by making the last payment into it. If this was the case, I would recommend using all or part of the lake of cash that you have.

One last thing on dollar-cost averaging: make sure that you keep making the payments even if markets take a big fall. It is scary, but a major slump will get you investments at a better price, and it makes no sense, having purchased investments at high prices, to decline investments now that they are bargains. If anything, a major slump should be seen as lucky for you, and you should consider increasing your payments rather than reducing them. (I have often said to clients who have just cashed up that the best thing that could happen to them now was a bloody good crash!)

Three critical requirements for your portfolio

Regardless of the drawdown rate you decide to use, your money should be held in a way that meets three critical requirements:

1. Your money should be **liquid**. This means it is easy to buy and sell the investments that you have in your retirement fund. That way you can get in and out quickly and without too much cost. This is important for retirees who may need cash or may have a need to get into or out of a market at any time. After all, retirees are spending both investment returns and capital, and you have to be able to draw regularly. It means that most of your investments should be in listed markets (e.g. the sharemarket or fixed interest securities that are listed) and that your holdings in all asset classes should be in bigger companies, or securities which are frequently traded (often, smaller companies that are listed on the sharemarket are not frequently traded and so the investments cannot always be liquidated at a particular time). In my view, this precludes investing in things like property syndicates. One of the big advantages of listed property (as opposed to syndicates) is that they can be sold and bought on the sharemarket at pretty much any time. It also precludes continuing to own all or part of your business and investing in private equity funds, which lock up your investment for a period of years.

2. You should probably be in a **balanced fund** at the start of retirement, although you may move to a more conservative position as time goes on. A balanced fund is generally one which has about 50% of its holdings in shares and listed property and 50% in fixed interest in cash. This applies whether you are investing in a managed fund, through a financial adviser or you are building the portfolio yourself. Building a portfolio is covered in the second part of this book. In retirement, I think it critical that you do not take on more risk than that of a balanced fund.
3. Your money should be **diversified**. You need to invest in all asset classes and to own a number of different investments within each asset class. After all, you may be retired for 30 years or more and, during that time, anything may happen in terms of economic and market events. Suffice to say the need for diversification (as well as liquidity) precludes owning a rental property, where this is the main or only asset you own and where the plan is to simply live on the rent. It also precludes continuing to own the family business or continuing to own the farm even when it is leased to someone. All these sorts of things concentrate your wealth to just one area and, in doing so, increase risk to an unacceptable level. Concentrating your assets like this also means you will not have any money invested offshore, something that you will see in Part 2 of this book is essential.

You should plan to draw a set, calculated amount, a percentage of your savings, when you first go into retirement. This amount will be calculated on an annual basis even though you may draw money to live on a fortnightly basis.

A well-diversified, liquid portfolio (and drawing a percentage from this each year) leads to investing in companies that will give the best returns for the risk regardless of whether those returns come from capital growth or dividends. This makes investment neutral — you are not biased towards any particular form of return, dividends or capital gain, and investment comes down to finding the best risk-adjusted return. Many people scour investment markets looking for the best dividends, which stops them buying excellent companies that do not pay dividends.

Diversification not only makes investment simpler but the management of your money in retirement becomes easier: provided you strike the right drawdown amount and investment returns are about normal, you have a higher chance of having enough money throughout retirement than if you simply chase investments which provide higher dividend or interest payments.

Instead of some of the more eccentric investment approaches, the right way is for you to establish a diversified portfolio and then draw a calculated amount, which you use to live on.

Drawdown rate

Drawdown rates are calculated on the basis that you have a conventional portfolio spread across all asset classes, which is exposed to dozens (maybe hundreds, even thousands) of different securities. Usually this will be a balanced portfolio (roughly 50% in shares and listed property with 50% in fixed interest and cash) but some people may have a conservative portfolio (approximately 70% in fixed interest and cash with 30% in shares and listed property).

The drawdown rate that you select (see chapter 4) is a percentage of your total portfolio at the start of retirement and it is a calculation for how much you will draw to live on each year.

Although the drawdown rate is calculated as an annual amount, you take out the money at time intervals that suit your money management best. Some people like this fortnightly — perhaps on the same day as NZ Super (which is also paid fortnightly) or perhaps in the week that NZ Super is not paid so that you have money coming in every week. Others may like to set it up so that it comes monthly — they may have been paid monthly all their working lives and are very used to receiving their incomes like that.

If you have your investments managed by a financial adviser, bank or brokerage house, you will be able to draw on your portfolio at a time of your convenience. Some managed funds may have difficulty with shorter term, regular withdrawals although most KiwiSaver funds are now set up to allow regular drawings for people over 65.

However, whatever the timing of your withdrawals, the drawdown rate is always expressed as a percentage of the funds that you have in the portfolio at the start of retirement, and this percentage is the total amount that you are drawing on an annual basis. For example, if you were planning to drawdown $20,000 each year, you could draw that monthly ($1,666 each month) or quarterly ($5,000 every three months).

Nevertheless, for planning purposes and to select a safe drawdown rate, you need to think on an annual basis. This would mean that if you had investment capital of $500,000 and you wanted $20,0000 each year, you would have a 4% drawdown rate ($20,0000 being 4% of $500,000).

The drawdown rate is the amount that you are going to spend — it is the amount that you receive after tax is paid. Almost all New Zealand funds that you might invest in are Portfolio Investment Entities (PIEs), and these will pay all the tax for you, provided you give the fund your correct prescribed investor rate (PIR). Those who are investing through a financial adviser may still have to do a tax return, but the adviser should give you an annual statement which will make that relatively easy. In any event, the amount of drawdown as calculated in the next chapter is assumed to be after fees and tax.

Drawdown methods to beware of

There are people who set out to spend only the cash returns that they get from a portfolio and nothing else. These cash returns —

from dividends and interest payments — will necessarily be less than those who are drawing regularly using a set drawdown rate. That's because those who use a set drawdown rate are spending all returns, capital gains as well as dividends and interest payments.

The idea of just using cash returns from interest payments, rents and dividends is probably a throwback to the days when it was common for people in retirement to put all their money with the bank and to spend the interest but leave the capital intact. Although people today can have a diversified portfolio, many still plan to spend just the income that derives from it. This ignores returns from capital gains and often leads them to chase riskier or poorly performing investments simply because they have high dividend yields or interest rates.

Chasing income investments leads to two main problems:

1. Income will be relatively poor because interest payments and dividends are now relatively low. Somebody who was starting to invest for cash income today will find that they have fairly lean pickings. We all know that interest rates are low, whether they come from bank deposits or fixed interest. However, dividends from shares and listed property are now also relatively low — dividends have not fallen but the price of shares and listed property have risen, meaning that the yield is lower.

2. Investing for cash income can drive some bad investment behaviour. If you plan to spend the cash from the portfolio (dividends and interest payments), you will naturally look for investments that pay higher interest or higher dividends. This is dangerous: such investments, whether shares, fixed interest or deposits, are likely to carry more risk and/or be poorer investments. The quest for cash returns was a good part of the Finance Company debacle in New Zealand in 2009, which ended with the Global Financial Crisis. Older people especially invested in finance companies because they paid a little more interest (not all that much more in some cases, but enough to attract retirees who saw a few additional

weekly dollars). The finance companies were built on poor foundations and most ended up broke. Chasing companies with high dividends may not be quite as bad but it does push people away from buying shares in companies like Amazon (which currently pays no dividend but, over the last 24 years since it listed, has given returns of 37% p.a.) and towards companies with little growth prospects. Choosing investments solely (or even largely) on their ability to pay dividends is not a good idea!

Other drawdown ideas

I have frequently met people who have told me their retirement plans features rental property. This plan is to purchase a rental property, spend 20 years repaying the mortgage and then use the rent from the property to fund their retirements. For people in their forties, this all seems a good idea because it handles both the accumulation and decumulation phases in one fell swoop.

However, simply owning a rental property in retirement and relying on that for decumulation is not a good idea. It flies in the face of two of the critical requirement for decumulation that are set out above: a rental property is neither a liquid investment nor is it a diversified one.

In fact, it is a very concentrated investment and if a big majority of your retirement investment capital is in this property and you own little else you could strike trouble:
- Rental property may not perform as well as it has in the past (recent government measures which extended the Brightline test and removed the tax deductibility of interest could decrease returns and greater compliance could reduce cash returns).
- A big concentration of your wealth in rental property excludes having money in other asset classes, and especially stops you from having a significant proportion of your retirement

- investments offshore.
- It is hard to draw on capital. The rents may continue to flow and these, along with NZ Super may meet your basic expenses, but to get at your capital if needed, will almost certainly require a sale of the property.
- When all costs are factored in, residential rental property does not really give a great deal of income.

I would make similar comments to those who have a business and plan to try to keep their business when they 'retire'. This plan may involve putting in managers or a business partner but, if the business's value makes up a large proportion of the retiree's wealth, it runs afoul of the two requirements for liquidity and diversification. It also does not allow for any kind of proper retirement. If you own a business, it is hard not to have at least some involvement and that involvement will likely be more than you want at times and may end up giving you continuous worry and work.

As you will see in the second part of this book, I see no alternative to a conventional diversified portfolio, probably one that is balanced (i.e. 50% is in growth assets and 50% in income assets).

I reckon #4 — Be prepared for inflation

Inflation is not the bogeyman that it was in the 1970s and 1980s. Around the world, central banks have been keeping inflation in check as one of their most important remits, with many required to keep it around 2% p.a. Provided that they are successful at keeping inflation at these sorts of levels, there may be little need for you to keep taking more from your portfolio to account for inflation.

Most studies show that your consumption will start to reduce as you get further into retirement and that means less requirement for income. This 'lower income' may take the form of drawing the same nominal amount (perhaps 5% of the starting portfolio) so that the spending power reduces with inflation. The key idea here is that you do not inflate the amount that you are drawing, which will allow you to draw more at the beginning.

Moreover, most Kiwis have a part of their income that is already inflation proofed — NZ Super. NZ Super is adjusted for inflation every six months and this makes retirees less vulnerable to inflation. This is especially so for those who have less income from investments and who have a higher proportion of their entire income coming from NZ Super. A couple who has $33,000 p.a. coming from NZ Super and $10,000 p.a. from investments is much less vulnerable to inflation than a couple who has $33,000 p.a. from NZ Super but $50,000 p.a. from investments.

Nevertheless, you cannot ignore inflation — it always has the potential to return and do to retirees what it did in the past (i.e. take from those who lent their money to the banks, and gave to those who borrowed from banks). Inflation is yet another reason why you should have a diversified portfolio. Some asset classes do better than others in times of high inflation: shares and property tend to do well, while fixed interest and cash do badly. I reckon that inflation is something we always need to be ready for, and we do that by owning a range of different investments some of which will get us through much better than others.

CHAPTER 4
Your Drawdown Rate

Decision time. You have cracked open the nest egg, counted up what is in there and now you have it well invested. Now you need to decide: how much will you be able to take from your investment to be able to live well and make your money last as long as you do?

This is a hard decision: remember that you are unlikely to be able to simply take the income from dividends and interest payments: these returns will almost certainly be too low for this. Instead, you will need to take a set proportion from a diversified portfolio regardless of the returns that you get and, almost, regardless of what happens. This decision on 'the set proportion of your portfolio' (i.e. your rate of drawdown) is both hard and important.

It is hard, and the hardest thing of all is that there are two conflicting goals:
1. The desire to be able to spend as much as you can to enjoy some of the good things in life during retirement.
2. The desire to protect your money from running out and the fear you will spend your final years in penury.

These two goals weigh heavily against each other. They largely depend on how long you think you will live and investment returns. The risk is that you will get this calculation completely wrong and either outlive your savings or leave a lot of your savings unspent.

As well as these conflicting goals, there is a third problem: you need to have steady, consistent drawing. You cannot simply take from the portfolio the total returns that you get each year and spend that amount. Investment volatility means that if you try to do that, there will be times when you could live like a king and times when you would not live at all. The rules of thumb and your own planning need to give amounts that you ought to be able to draw each year, even with the ups and downs of the markets.

Your drawdown rate will likely be 4–6% p.a. of the capital you have at the point of retirement. The rate you finally choose will be based on your personal situation and will take into account things like your likely life expectancy and perceived investment returns in the first few years of retirement.

There is no guarantee that you will get your drawdown perfectly right — there are too many unknowns for that. We all want to draw as much as we can to live as well as we can. We also want the money to last just the right amount of time. However, there are several variables that need to be estimated and none of these is likely to turn out exactly as planned. These variables include your longevity, investment returns and inflation, and you cannot expect to predict any of these perfectly over a 20- or 30-year period.

Your drawdown rate will always have to be an approximation and needs to be monitored and possibly changed over the decades that make up your retirement years. The right drawdown rate is not a precise science — there are simply too many unknowns for that.

Fortunately, there have been others who have gone before — the rate at which you can draw down on your savings in retirement has been a known problem for decades and various people have done work to help people just like you. These people have calculated guidelines that make sense; they give varying rates that you can use depending on your circumstances and the degree to which you seek the safety of knowing that the money will last, or the desire to spend more heavily.

Drawdown calculations

All drawdown rates should be calculated by looking at five main things:

1. Likely investment returns
2. Likely tax rates
3. Future inflation rates
4. Life expectancy
5. Likely expenditure patterns

All of these things have to be considered over very long periods of time and, of course, we do not really know what the future holds. Any of these five factors could be higher or lower than what could reasonably be used in drawdown calculations. For example, we can look at what investment returns have been like over long periods of time through history, and make some adjustments based on the current climate. We can do this intelligently with all of the information available but that will not mean that it will work out perfectly — one or more of these five factors are likely to go awry to a greater or lesser extent.

The drawdown rates that are given below are an approximation and, given that we can never perfectly know the future, they will not be perfectly correct. Nevertheless, they are the best we have and one of them should form the basis of the amount you will take from your investments. The rates set out below are an awful lot better than a simple guess!

The two big variables that are most important (and unknown!) are your future investment returns and your life expectancy.

Investment returns

This is something that you need to be very careful about. Certainly, achieving higher returns will make the money last longer or give you the ability to draw more. Mostly people should use a balanced portfolio at the start of retirement, and perhaps move to a conservative portfolio as retirement goes on. Naming a portfolio in this way is simple shorthand to indicate their asset allocation: a balanced fund has about 50% in growth assets while a conservative fund will have about 30% in growth assets.

The allocation of growth assets compared to income assets will likely establish the returns that you get and the volatility that you will endure more than anything else. Because of this you need to be very careful of making changes.

Yes, you could get higher returns by moving to a growth fund (75% in growth assets). That may seem like an easy fix to make the money last longer or to be able to increase your income. However, that would inevitably increase volatility and have you extremely vulnerable to sequencing risk (see page 65). Few people using an investment portfolio for retirement income would (or should!) take much, if any, more risk than having a balanced portfolio.

However, what you may do to increase returns a little is to take advice and, probably, have someone manage your money for you. Similarly, you could use a fund that you know to give good investment performance. These things can increase returns a little, but do not have expectations that are too high, because it is asset allocation that usually makes the big difference to investment performance.

As a matter of guidance, the Financial Markets Authority (FMA) calculates that the investment returns on a balanced portfolio ought to be about 3.5% after tax and fees. The rules of thumb for drawdown are greater than this because you are drawing on capital as well as investment returns.

Life expectancy

The time that savings will have to last is not dictated solely by when the end may come — just as important is when you are going to start to draw down on savings. I have explored the idea of delaying retirement for a while and said that it can make a great deal of difference to the amount that you will have in retirement (albeit at the cost of more years in some kind of work, which may not be your preference). A key part of carrying on working, even if part-time, means that you delay the start of drawdown, making for fewer years that you will need investment capital.

You should remember that if there are two of you, the money has to last for the longest life. It could be that although you may have a shorter life than average, your partner may live to a grand old age and require enough money to keep him or her in champagne for years past the average.

All of the rules of thumb are designed to give you rough guidelines. They work on averages and, whatever the average life expectancy is for someone your age, that is not necessarily your life expectancy. You may have reached 65 and now, as a woman, could expect to reach ninety. However, you cannot be confident that you will make ninety, nor can you be confident that you will make eighty: ever since I hit 65, I have become aware that you are only as good as your last doctor's visit — at a certain age, your last diagnosis is the important one.

Personalise your drawdown rate

None of the drawdown rates set out below should be followed slavishly. In my view, they are a good basis for you to personalise your own drawdown rates. We all have different situations, and we all have different goals, wants and needs.

To meet those goals, wants and needs it seems to me to be perfectly reasonable to adopt one of the drawdown rates that is set out below but then to draw either a little more or a little less depending on how you want to live in retirement. These adjustments could be based on any number of factors that are personal to you:

- You are especially concerned about outliving your money and spending your final years in penury. You might, therefore, draw less than one of the rates given.

- You do not think your life expectancy will be great. You could, therefore, live it up and spend more.
- You could decide that your expenditure late in retirement will be much lower. You could, therefore, increase your expenditures at the beginning of retirement.
- You may want to leave more substantial inheritances. To accommodate these, you might lower your drawdown rate.
- You may be going into an early retirement (perhaps in your fifties). You would need your money to last longer and so lower your drawdown rate.

There are plenty of circumstances that could mean you make adjustments to the rate to some extent: perhaps moving 1–2% from the rule of thumb (say from 4% to 5%). I would caution that you do not step too far away from one of the four established drawdown rates set out below unless you have good advice or you have some circumstance that takes you out of the ordinary.

The four drawdown rates

These four drawdown rates come from the New Zealand Society of Actuaries (NZSA). They have prepared a paper (which I hope they will continue to update) describing each drawdown rate, who it is suitable for and the probablility of you outliving your money. It can be found at: https://actuaries.org.nz/decumulation-rules-of-thumb-report-update-november-2020/

The most recent paper is dated November 2020 and is an update of a paper that was first prepared in 2017. The paper makes some of the following assumptions:
- You invest in a Conservative fund;
- Kiwi retirees should now plan to live to 90–95 years;
- Lower interest rates mean that investment returns will likely be lower in coming years; and
- The amounts you take from your investments are tax-paid.

Lower interest rates and greater life expectancy mean that the amount that you can draw down safely has reduced in recent years. The one thing I would query in the NZSA assumptions is that retirees invest as conservative investors (defined as someone who has 30% of a portfolio or fund in shares and property and 70% in fixed interest and cash). In my experience, most retirees use a balanced fund, and it is balanced funds that are usually found in most drawdown-rate commentary.

While these sorts of drawdown rates can be found elsewhere, it is most helpful that the NZSA has done this work and published it. Most other drawdown rates that you see have been done in other countries (especially the USA) and they can have quite different returns, longevity and tax rates, which could make the amount that you can draw different from a safe rate in New Zealand. I do hope that the NZSA will continue to update these rates; it is very, very useful to have these rules done by Kiwis for Kiwis.

The four drawdown rates that you can choose from are:
1. The 4% rule
2. The 6% rule
3. The fixed date rule
4. The life expectancy rule

These are all rules of thumb, and like all rules of thumb they are not personalised at all. A rule of thumb is an approximate method of doing or calculating something, a rough and ready estimation. In absence of personalised advice, these rules of thumb are the best that we have, and it is reasonable for you to base your drawings from them. However, do apply some common sense and get some advice. The personalisation of your drawdown rate could be the difference between spending a wonderful retirement with plenty, or living solely on New Zealand Super.

1. The 4% rule

The 4% rule is given the most space in this book, not because I think it ought to be followed by most people, but because it is best known and most used (in fact, I would seldom blindly follow the 4% rule even though I have often used it for planning purposes).

The 4% rule was devised by William Bengen in 1994. Bengen was a financial adviser from the US and recognised that most people do not have a tame actuary who they keep about the house to advise them of their retirement drawdown rate — he wanted a rule of thumb that we could all use to guide us. Bengen used 50 years of data (from 1926 to 1976) to back test his idea and using this he published his rule. Since 1994, there have been many others who have run numbers to prove or disprove the rule — on the whole it has stood up very well.

The 4% rule says that you can draw 4% of your total savings in the first year, increasing that amount to account for inflation each year. This means that if you had $500,000, in the first year you could draw $20,000, in the second year you could draw $20,400 (assuming inflation was 2%), in the third year $20,808 and so on for 30 years. The 4% rule assumes that you invest in a balanced portfolio and says that at that rate of drawing, someone who started at age 65 would have a high probability of the money lasting to age 95.

This gives you a steady income across retirement. The portfolio might be volatile (actually, it will be volatile, after all the portfolio or fund has 50% in shares and listed property) as it goes up and down with the markets, but you can draw a reliable amount out and use it to live on. As such, the rule of 4% gives us the best of both worlds: we can invest in a portfolio that will give us decent returns (much better than term deposits) and, ignoring the volatility, you can carry on drawing out your $20,000 plus inflation for 30 years.

That is investment Nirvana: a steady income from a volatile portfolio.

However, we do have to be careful with this: Bengen never said that the money will last — he said that it had a high probability of lasting 30 years. We know that it may last more than this and it may last less. We also know that you might last more or less than 30 years. We must come back to the idea that this is a rule of thumb and should only be treated as a guide.

Since Bengen published the rule of 4%, it has faced controversy. Despite only being a guide, some of the comments have been:

- The period which Bengen used (1926–1976) included a period of very high inflation;
- Bengen did not deduct fees from investment returns;
- Life expectancy is changing;
- Investment returns are likely to be higher than 1926–1976 because of our tech explosion;
- Investment returns are likely to be lower than 1926–1976 because of low interest rates;
- Bengen only used US data;
- The rule is not personalised (rules of thumb are not usually personalised);
- The rule is too rigid (most rules are); and
- Bengen's confidence that the money would last was near 100% — maybe 75% would be fine.

I picked out these bullet points almost at random to show the range of arguments in all sorts of forums. Some would make you think that 4% of your starting portfolio's value is too little, some that it is too much. This has long been the way of the 4% rule — it has always been controversial.

Bengen is now 73 years old and has retired to Arizona. He continues to do research and run numbers: in a 2021 interview with *Barron's* magazine, Bengen said that he thought most people could safely go to a 4.5% drawdown rate — i.e. he has increased his drawdown rate.

I also note that the New Zealand Society of Actuaries (NZSA) in its paper dated November 2020 shows that the 4% rule works quite well. Their paper shows that a 4% drawdown rate is 'almost certain' to last until age 90, and 'is probable' to be good until age 95.

My difficulties with the 4% rule

Although I think that the 4% rule is a good place to start, I have some concerns about it:

It gives the same amount or income each year, which takes no account of changing spending patterns in retirement. As you can see in chapter 2, expenditure in retirement is usually higher at the beginning of retirement, but gradually reduces as we move through our seventies and into our eighties.

New Zealand investment returns are generally higher than those in the US. Although you will have some global investments in your portfolio, the bulk of your investments will be in New Zealand. The higher returns in New Zealand mean that you ought to be able to draw more than 4%.

Many people do not retire at 65 years, and probably do not need their money to last thirty years — for someone retiring at age 70, the money probably only needs to last 20 or 25 years, and their time of high spending when they first retire will probably be shorter. This will mean that they can spend more than 4% in those early years of retirement.

Variations on the 4% rule

My response to the 4% rule as a financial adviser was to personalise it to at least some extent. This personalisation usually meant higher drawings than 4% and would be based on factors like:

1. An increase to the amount to be drawn because someone has shorter life expectancy. This may be because of retiring later than age 65 or because of health.
2. An increase to the amount to be drawn because people will be happy to use the house for a reverse annuity mortgage late in retirement.
3. A decrease in the amount to be drawn because they want to leave bigger inheritances.
4. An increase or decrease in the drawdown rate because

investment returns are expected to be lower or higher.
5. A decrease in the amount to be drawn because the client is deeply fearful of running out of money.
6. A decrease to the amount to be drawn because the client is young (some were retiring in their fifties and need the money to last 40 or more years).

I think all the evidence points to the 4% rule being a reasonable (if conservative) starting point, or as a minimum to be taken from a portfolio. However, I think that most people could afford to draw more from their investments, especially in those early years of retirement when we are most active and eager to do things. I also think that most people can afford to personalise their drawdown rates for their own circumstances.

Remember that Bengen came up with quite a rigid drawdown, one that was the same at the end of retirement as it was at the start. I think that few people will be doing the same things and spending the same money at the end of retirement as they did at the start.

In any event, people are not stupid and will generally adjust their lifestyles as needs arise. Most retired people have spent their lives altering their expenditures to their incomes. I cannot see why at some magical age of 65 they would continue to draw down even when times are straightened. It seems to me that retired people could be relied on to tighten their belts a little if there was a prolonged period of severe economic difficulty leading to some years of poor investment returns. Moreover, I am very keen on people holding a 'lake of cash' outside and in addition to their portfolios as reserve funds to tide you over a difficult period (see page 64).

For my money, the 4% rule is safe — using that, you would be very unlucky to run out of money before 30 years. It is probably too safe for most people, but you could start out on that rate if you can and draw a bit more if things go well for a few years. However, it is probably too safe — you are probably leaving some spending and good activities on the table.

The 4% rule is suitable for:
- Those who want to know that their money will last, and those who would like a fairly high chance of leaving inheritances beyond the house. It is especially good for those who retire at age 65, whereas those who retire at (say) 70, could afford to take more.
- The 4% is almost certainly the safest of all the drawdown rates, and probably the most predictable. It has some drawbacks as outlined: the income is constant through retirement (even though your expenditure is not), you have to keep an eye on inflation to raise the amount, and you may get close to the end and think you have left too much money on the table (so to speak).

2. The 6% rule

This rule has you drawing 6% of your original amount of savings, but not increasing it with inflation as is done in the 4% rule. This means that if you had $500,000, you could draw $30,000 each year. As you would imagine, taking more income to live on means the money will not last as long: according to the NZSA figures, drawing 6% will 'almost certainly' get you to age 82 (i.e. 17 years of retirement), and you will have a 50% chance of your money lasting until age 85 (19 years of retirement). After these ages, there is a fairly good chance that you will have to live on NZ Super alone or start to tap into the value of the house.

Some people may use the 6% rate at the beginning and plan to reduce the amount after some period (a period of good living!). It could be that after 8–10 years (a time that probably allows for some good years but when expenditure could be starting to fall) you reduce your drawings quite sharply. Such a plan may have a reverse mortgage or some other use of the house as a back-up.

Like the 4% rule, the 6% rule is very simple (even simpler than the 4% rule because you are not having to increase it with the

Consumer Price Index). It is a known amount, and you will have a lot of income in the early years of retirement. The downside is, of course, that it is quite likely you will watch your savings go to zero (which may be a very uncomfortable feeling).

There is a risk, of course, when you do not plan to increase your income with inflation. Over the 17-year period that you are drawing at 6%, there is a reasonable chance that inflation will get away again — and that could leave you exposed. However, your NZ Super will be rising at about the same rate as inflation and, in any event, at some point, your income needs will start to reduce. This gradual reduction in needs probably covers inflation.

The 6% rule is suitable for quite a lot of people:
- Those who carry on in work after age 65 and who do not touch their savings (except perhaps to add to them) until a later date. For example, someone retiring at age 70 could be more confident that their money will last.
- Those with a shorter life expectancy.
- Those who really want to live it up in the early years of retirement.
- Those who plan for a sharp fall in expenditure about 10 years through retirement.
- Those who have no care about whether or not they leave any sort of inheritance.
- Those who are confident they can live on NZ Super, possibly supplemented by drawing down on the equity they have in their homes.

It is less suitable for:
- Those who go into retirement early.
- Those who are likely to worry a lot about whether their money will last.

3. The fixed date rule

This rule is a bit different: you figure out how many years you want your money to last, and then take out an amount equivalent to the capital that you have at any time divided by the number of years before the end date.

For example, let's say that you retire at 65 and expect that you want your savings to last until age 90 (either because you think that is when you will die or because you think you can live on NZ Super from then on). You start retirement with $500,000 and need it to last 25 years, and so, in the first year you take $20,000, being a 25th of $500,000. This leaves you with $480,000. The fund grows, so, a year later, when you come to see what you can draw, the fund is now at $504,000 (a fairly good year because you got an investment return of 5%). There are now 24 years until the 'end' and so you can take $21,000. The following year the fund is at $420,000 (a bad year for investments) and you can take $18,260, being $420,000 divided by 23.

The key thing about this rule is that unlike the 4% rule or the 6% rule, you do not have a standard, constant amount each year; you will have to live on what the numbers show, and this could be under or over last year's amount, depending on returns. The other important things to note is that there is no allowance for inflation — like the 6% rule, which is not inflated, you are at the mercy of inflation.

The NZSA's calculations show that this has a very good chance of getting you from age 65 through to age 90. After that, assuming that you follow the rule right through, you are on your own with your NZ Super and, maybe, a house.

The fixed date rule is suitable for:
- Those who are confident they will not need income beyond NZ Super after a certain age.
- Those not concerned with inheritances.
- Those who do not want to make complicated calculations (there is a calculation to make but it is easy and only once a year).

It is not so suitable for:

- Those who need a steady, predictable income.

4. Life expectancy rule

This is the most complicated rule and, as such, will probably not suit a lot of people. Our life expectancy changes as we age. As an extreme example, at birth the life expectancy of a girl is about 82 years. However, if she makes it through to age 65 years, having survived birth, childhood disease, teenage years on her motorbike, giving birth to her own children, driving her own car, etc., she will have a life expectancy of nearly 90. As she gets older, her life expectancy continues to increase, regrettably, not forever.

This rule allows retirees to take an amount equalling the value of their savings divided by the number of years they expect to have left. In the first year, because a man would have 22 years life expectancy (age 65 through to 87), from $500,000 he could take $22,700 ($500,000 divided by 22). This would continue through retirement, being updated each year according to actuarial tables that will show how long he has left.

The NZSA paper shows the amount taken reducing almost from the start but the money lasting well off to about 100 years of age (although it gets to be quite low from about age 85 years). Under this rule, you will always have an income even though it will be a very small income late in life.

Finding your life expectancy each year to recast the numbers will be a barrier for a lot of people and I suspect this will be little used.

The life expectancy rule is suitable for:
- Those who want more money at the start of retirement and to have some money (albeit probably very small) no matter how long they live.
- Those who do not care about leaving any inheritances.

This is not suitable for:
- Those who want steady income.
- Those who do not want to make slightly complicated calculations each year.

Creating your own spreadsheet

There will be people reading this who would be quite capable of preparing a spreadsheet that would cover their retirement, and which, with a few adjustments, would show a reasonable drawdown rate. This would have the advantage that the drawdown rate would be personalised: you could put in your expectations of expenditure over the course of retirement. Moreover, and even better still, you could monitor this and make adjustments as the markets perform well or badly, as your expenditures rise of fall, and according to you latest doctor's visit.

The problem with this is that you need to be privy to some key assumptions: life expectancy, investment returns, expected inflation rates (if you are going to keep up with inflation), and your expected future expenditures. I have seen people do spreadsheets as I am suggesting but, although the spreadsheets themselves are good, the assumptions have been a long way out. From a technical spreadsheet point of view, the job is not too hard; from an assumption point of view, it is quite difficult.

Getting advice

There are a lot of things in finance that we take advice on — our investments, mortgages, insurance — but people seldom get advice on our drawdown rate. Getting advice is important, not just because you may run out of money, or you might leave behind far more than you hoped. It is important too because some people live in fear that they will run out or are not living as well as they could; they just do not know if they are doing it right or not.

When you consider this, you recognise just how valuable the NZSA rules of thumb are.

However, as I have shown above, these rates are not personalised and are a bit rough and ready. They do not take account of anything that might change in your personal circumstances, nor any economic or market event that could take place tonight, next year or in a decade. Such things could very quickly change the safe drawdown rate for you.

This is an area where some advice could be invaluable. That advice could come from one of three sources:

1. **An actuary.** This would be the best person to advise you as this kind of thing is what actuaries are for. They are (obviously enough) trained in maths and statistics but on a day-to-day basis are working in finance, economics, policy, risk management, demography and behavioural science. They pull all of these different disciplines together to draw their conclusions and make their evaluations. However, to calculate a drawdown rate for you personally would not be quick and easy — I asked an actuary how long this would take and got 'about a day' as an answer. This would probably mean the cost is $2,000–$3,000 and, although it could be money well spent, I doubt that many people would pay it.

2. **A financial adviser.** Some financial advisers could give very useful advice on drawdown rates, while others will not. To be fair, this is not core business for most; only a few have any way of being paid for such work. Financial advisers tend to be interested in (and follow) investment markets or insurance and mortgages. In some ways, it is hardly fair to expect them to be expert in drawdown rates as well. Nevertheless, there are financial advisers who would be perfectly capable of calculating a suitable drawdown rate for you, could get fairly accurate assumptions and would have enough experience to do a good job of it. How and how much they might charge for this I do not know.

3. **A drawdown fund.** Again, with the caveat that I am writing from a position as a shareholder and Director of the Lifetime Retirement Income, I would say that a specialist drawdown fund takes a lot of the worry out of this whole area. In fact, Lifetime Retirement Income is established to take the uncertainty out of those two big financial questions in retirement: how should you invest, and how much can you draw down? Lifetime's actuary has developed a model so that you will know your drawdown rate and then, on your birthday each year, Lifetime checks to see if there should be any variation. I think this an excellent and most useful service (but the I would say that, wouldn't I?).

My take on drawdown rates

There is no simple answer to your drawdown rate. Even if you had personalised advice from an actuary, the drawdown number would still not be precise: in the absence of your medical records (and maybe even with them), the assessment of your life expectancy would probably only be an average — and you will probably not be average. Moreover, investment returns for the next 20 or 30 years cannot be precise. Over time, tax rates may change.

If I had $500,000 and retired at age 70, I think I would draw 6% at the start (i.e. $30,000 p.a. or about $600 per week) to supplement my NZ Super. I would plan to reduce this after a few years and would expect by age 80, to be living on about $20,000 p.a. or $400 per week on top of NZ Super. Expenditure would have to fall further as I moved through my eighties, and, maybe by the end I would be living on very pleasant memories of those early years of retirement.

On the whole, I would favour either the 4% rule or the 6% rule for their simplicity and for the well-beaten path they provide. Of the two, I prefer the 6% rule because it allows higher expenditure at the beginning of retirement but, that said, it may require some variations or adjustments. If in doubt, adopt one of the methods and make some kind of adjustments at the start. Then, as you go through retirement you should try to track how you are going as closely as possible.

For some people in some circumstances, I might make adjustments. Given the fall in expenditure in retirement and the fact that most people underspend, it would probably not do too much harm if you took (say) 1% extra (5% instead of 4%, if you are following the 4% rule).

Any variations you make to a rule should be based on the following principles:

- The older you are when you retire, the more you can take.
- The older you are, the less likely you are to need to inflate what you take.
- The more nervous you are about running out of money, the less you should take.
- If you invest in a conservative fund (rather than balanced), the less you can take.
- As you will see below, I reckon that you should take only what you need, not what you can.

I reckon #5 — Keep an eye on your expenditure
Draw what you need, not what you can. There are people who find that their drawdown for their portfolio is more than what they need to live well. If, for example, they draw 6%, they may find this is more than enough, perhaps because they are doing some work, or their expenditure is lower than expected. In this situation it is easy to simply spend more: spending easily rises to meet (or even exceed) income.

If this is you, keep a rein on your expenditure. Remember that rules of thumb like the 4% rule are a guide and, in some ways, represent the maximum that you can safely draw. There could be any manner of things coming down the track towards you — a period of very high inflation which raises costs, a long period of poor investment returns, or both of these things coming together. Moreover, things can happen in your life that may see a sharp increase in costs — perhaps a medical emergency, or some other issue in the family.

Do not be lured into higher expenditure because there is a period of very high returns, or just because you can. The world has a way of levelling things out and reverting to the mean — a good period is often followed by a not-so-good period.

CHAPTER 5
Other Sources of Income

For the most part, this chapter concerns those who have not saved quite enough to give them the lifestyle they want. In some respects, people who are in this situation — they want to retire but just cannot make the numbers work — are on hold for retirement. They need to keep bringing in some income but, hopefully, achieve a semi-retirement that does not have the pressure of their previous full-time work.

If you are in this situation you need to go on a treasure hunt, looking everywhere for extra income that you can piece together to make an acceptable whole.

Income in retirement can come from:
- New Zealand Super
- work
- a micro-business
- the house

As in just about every part of planning, there are compromises to be made. For example, renting out a room means doing some work and leads to a loss of privacy; working part-time negates the very thing you were trying to achieve (retirement, by definition, means stopping work).

Nevertheless, as you look for income and consider options, there is always that other possibility: carrying on in work as you are. The thing that I keep coming back to is the kind of life that you want. This means considering exactly what you mean by 'retirement', and how you want to live your life. After all, this is your life and your retirement and, therefore, your compromises. For example, if you would be happier with a little more money from a little work than you would be with less money and no work, then you should do it.

Buying time

Some extra income may let you buy some time. Although it may not give you everything that you want from retirement, things like working a little or renting out a room early in 'retirement' should mean that your drawdown rate is less, or, perhaps, you will not need to draw on savings at all. This buys time for your savings to grow a bit more and, just as important, there will be less time for which your savings will be required. This, when you do start to use your savings, will mean a higher drawdown rate.

Retirement should not be considered one long homogenous stage of life. In fact, retirement has several stages each of which requires different amounts of expenditure, which will come from different amounts of income. It is critical to realise that your income requirements are unlikely to remain the same across all of retirement.

The things that you may have to do to provide income at the beginning of retirement will probably not continue right through the whole of retirement; you will probably not have to work part-time or continue to rent out a room when you are 85.

Moreover, continuing to earn income for some years should mean that you drawdown less from your investment portfolio. This means that your drawdown rate can rise later in retirement as the investment portfolio's value has not reduced as much.

In effect, earning income early in retirement buys time later in retirement: late in retirement you will have less need for income and, also, you will have a greater ability to draw from your portfolio.

Of course, this should come with a warning: continuing to work, run a micro-business or do short-term rentals may not be your idea of retirement. These kinds of things have a way of disrupting the things that you really want to do: you may have a shift at work on the day your grandson is born, or on the opening day of the fishing season. A need for additional income early in retirement may stop you doing the things that you always dreamed of doing. And, early on in retirement may be just that time that you should be doing them.

Another option could be to draw down more than planned from your investments. Instead of drawing 4% at the start of retirement (planning to draw this amount through all of retirement) you might draw 6%, knowing that at some point in the future you will have to reduce this (maybe quite sharply). Planning to draw more at the start of retirement so that you can live well will be an uncomfortable feeling for many — it seems almost irresponsible because you know that even if you do not completely run out of money, you will be scraping the bottom of the barrel at some point.

Still, many people need to make compromises and work around things until there is a reasonable plan that gives them most (if not all) of what they want.

It is worth looking at all the usual sources of income in a little more detail.

New Zealand Superannuation

NZ Super is the foundation for many people's retirement income. For a couple on the 'M' rate of tax (this is for those who have total income above $48,000 p.a.) the amount of NZ Super is approximately $35,000 p.a. (for a single person it is approximately $20,000 p.a.). This is not a lot of money but would provide a basic (very basic!) living. However, there are a lot of people who live on NZ Super and nothing else.

NZ Super is not means tested and is available to everyone legally resident in New Zealand and over 65. You must have lived in New

Zealand for at least 10 years since age 20 with five of those years in New Zealand since you turned 50. You have to apply for NZ Super, which you can do online or with a visit to your local WINZ office. When you have successfully applied, you will also get a Gold Card, which gives some discounts and things like free travel off-peak on public transport.

By global standards, NZ Super is very generous. As a universal pension scheme, it is very cheap to administer because NZ Super is simply paid out of Government funds. Although the NZ Super Fund (a.k.a. the Cullen fund) was set up in 2003 to help pay for NZ Super as baby boomers retired, today this stands at only $58 billion. Although this may sound a lot, the cost to the government of NZ Super on an annual basis is about $15 billion and growing. NZ Super is not a fully funded scheme and will have to continue to largely come out of taxes as they are collected.

The debate in New Zealand regarding whether NZ Super is affordable and can continue in its present form is ongoing. Politicians' pussy foot around it, but my guess is that it will continue pretty much as is for the foreseeable future. There are a lot of baby boomers and we vote!

I think you can make your plans and build NZ Super into them. Barring some catastrophe, it seems most likely to continue much as it is (although the age of entitlement may increase, and qualifying rules may change).

NZ Super — where does it fit in?

The most important features of NZ Super are:
- It is passive income — you do not have to do anything to get it other than stay in New Zealand for six months each year;
- It is regular and likely to continue come what may; and
- It is inflation adjusted.

While I am sure you do not want to live solely on NZ Super, it is indeed the foundation of most retirees' plans. Although there are a few retirees who give their NZ Super to the kids or to a charity, these people are, in fact, very rare (or, they still have a lot of work/business income beyond age 65 years). Most of us have NZ Super as a key component of our retirement income.

The fact that it is regular, and you need do nothing to get it, makes it unlike any of your other income (other than additional pensions a few people might have). NZ Super is unlike work, unlike a small business, unlike renting out a room, and unlike returns from your investment portfolio. It is not volatile, and it will hit your bank account as regularly as your salary once did.

NZ Super is adjusted each year to maintain the spending power of 66% of the average, ordinary-time wage for couples. The fact that it is effectively adjusted for inflation every year makes it even more certain — it will not get whittled away and diminished over time. Inflation is always a threat for retired people. The retired complained bitterly through the 1970s and 1980s when inflation ran riot, and most retirees had their money in bank deposits. Over the last 30 years or so, inflation has not been the problem it once was — partly because it has been a lot lower, partly because more people have invested smarter, and partly because NZ Super is hedged against inflation.

Nevertheless, you need to plan for a retirement of at least 30 years and, over that time, anything can happen — including a return of high inflation. Knowing that a proportion of your income (NZ Super) is hedged against inflation should be a great comfort.

Because NZ Super is so dependable, many people set it aside for certain costs. I know many people who use the NZ Super payment to pay for the basics (groceries, utilities and transport) or some other set of regular expenses (rates, insurance and groceries). I think this kind of money management can be very useful and, as I show below, can be taken further.

The important thing is that NZ Super is the most passive (least work), most reliable and inflation-proof income that you will have in retirement. That is why the great majority of retirees treasure it.

Working in retirement

Around 40% of people aged 65–69 are still in paid work. Of course, many do not simply stop work at age 69: something like 5800 Kiwis over age 80 are still working according to 2020 figures from Statistics NZ. A study in 2014 found that 71% of those who were working over the age of 65 believed that they had enough money; they were working for reasons other than financial.

If you plan to work while still getting NZ Super, you will have lots of company. The reasons are many and varied: people need the social contact, they find work interesting, they do not want to break the habits of a lifetime, and, for the sake of their relationship, one of them needs to get out of the house. Anyway, for some, while the extra money may not be strictly needed, it is still useful and is sometimes set aside for a particular purpose.

Then there are those who really do need the money — they cannot live on NZ Super alone; they cannot really afford to retire. These people are working because they have to — and probably doing the same old grind that they always have. If there is any comfort for these people, it is that their financial position ought to get better with time. If they have any savings, they will grow, and if they have a mortgage, that should reduce further.

Nevertheless, for a lot of older Kiwis, the outlook is fairly bleak.

Finding work

One thing that inspired my book *Twenty Good Summers* was that I realised quite a lot of friends and clients in their fifties were starting to get fed up with what they had been doing most of their working lives. Often in the professions, or with senior positions in companies and other organisations, or perhaps owning a business, they had worked hard in relatively stressful positions and needed a break. They did not necessarily want to completely stop and retire — a lot could not afford to do that — but they wanted to do something else, and to do less. That book gave them permission:

it showed them how they may well have enough to ease back into something different and have more relaxed (and healthier!) lives.

I know a good number of people (many were clients) who, on this basis, gave up their professions, sold the business or resigned their position to do other things. They looked for part-time work that was not as full-on as they had been doing.

However, although work was always part of the plan, it was sometimes not easy to find. These (often very capable) people found that ageism was alive and well in New Zealand. One friend who took this route left her profession, swearing she would never go back (ever!). She took a few months off then started to look for work but could find nothing. She even applied for a job flipping burgers at a local takeaway shop but was turned down because the rest of the staff would not want to work with a nana!

Such people who cannot find work are probably the minority. I know plenty of people who have taken jobs as tour bus drivers or who fill in at a shop to give the owner a break. They are very happy with what they are doing and would not go back to their previous high-stress life.

Working in retirement can be satisfying and rewarding. I do think it pays to line the work up before you retire, or at least know the kind of thing that you will do, if not the details of who you will work for and the hours you will work. I get a sense that many people find work in retirement by word of mouth, although I do know people who have applied for jobs and got them. When I go into a supermarket or other business, I cannot help noticing that there seem to be a lot of older people (my age!) working there.

I know people who work one or two days (or maybe half-days) a week. However, I also know people who work for a couple of months a year and have the rest of the year off. This may be seasonal work (like the grape harvest) or some other arrangement.

Finally, do not forget that even a relatively small amount of income from work can make a big difference to your finances in retirement. A small amount of work can substitute for a large amount of capital. If you apply the 4% rule, earning $10,000 from work means that you can have $250,000 less capital (i.e. you need $250,000 at a drawdown rate of 4% to get yourself $10,000). This is not strictly true, of course, because the capital continues to give you that income for 30 years and you are unlikely to work for that long. Nevertheless, as the numbers working in retirement show, some work has a lot of merit and can very usefully built into your plans.

A micro-business

In many respects a micro-business is different from working for someone else in retirement. The big difference is a micro-business is often done from home. Some people seem to have the knack of turning a hobby into a business or providing a service to people that they had often done free for friends and family. Pet walking or grooming, babysitting, crafts, guiding tourists are the kinds of things I see a lot of people with silver hair doing. In the past year, I have employed three people who were my age for handyman work around the house. Internet businesses are also quite common as are things like computer and TV set-ups (which one of these three 'retired' people did for me).

Again, these do not have to be big money makers. A small amount to supplement NZ Super and reduce your drawdown makes a big difference to your ability to do the things you want to do in retirement.

A micro-business may have some advantages over taking a part-time job. First, it may give more flexibility in terms of time. However, the idea of being your own boss may sound good but often gives less freedom than expected. Working for and by yourself does make you the boss but it also makes you the person who does everything else as well: marketing manager, bookkeeper, salesperson, debt collector and floor sweeper. And on top of that you still have to provide the service or goods to the customer. Yes, you may be able to choose your hours of work, but those hours may prove a lot longer than you bargained for.

Second, there can be tax benefits. Depending on the nature of the business things like home/office costs, your phone, car expense, etc. may be tax deductible. There are rules around this kind of thing: for instance, the enterprise has to be a proper business, not just a hobby. As such, you must have the intention to make a profit from your micro-business and there must also be a realistic probability that you will make a profit. You cannot turn your hobby into a pretend 'business' and claim expenses.

Nevertheless, people do make profits from micro-businesses, whether that is doing the make-up for bridal parties or making the cakes for the guests. It is worth considering the many things that you are good at and can teach — from teaching and guiding fly fishing to arranging people's travel itineraries, you may end up getting paid to do something you love.

The house

Your house is such a big part of your retirement plan I have devoted the next chapter to it (chapter 6). The important thing to recognise when planning your retirement is that your house is probably your most valuable asset. As such, there are opportunities to unlock the capital tied up in it and turn it into retirement income. These opportunities include:

- downsizing
- home equity release
- remortgaging for income
- selling and renting
- short-term rentals

Many older people stay on in the family home they have owned for some decades, knowing that it is too big and expensive to keep. Sometimes they hold on out of habit, sometimes because they have left it too long and cannot face the prospect of a shift. These same people may complain of being asset rich, cash poor — that is, they own a big house and not much else.

Being asset rich and cash poor is, in fact, a choice but this is something that needs to be thought about, and planned for, early in retirement, rather than when the big house starts to become a problem. After all, you probably have more capital tied up in the house than anything else, and this capital needs to be thought about and conscious decisions made about it just as you would for any other major asset.

> **I reckon #6 — Assess the benefits of continuing to work**
> Work gets a bad rap. Some people count the sleeps until they can retire and long for the day when they can walk out with no intention of coming back. That's fair enough — not all work is fun, and no work is fun all of the time. However, I do think that some people need to change their work — as we were repeatedly told at primary school, a change is as good as a holiday.
>
> Work can give structure to the day, social contact and promote a feeling of being useful. The money is important for many, but it is often other, less tangible things that keep people on the supermarket checkout counter on Tuesdays and Thursdays.
>
> Now well beyond 'retirement age', I have still not retired. Certainly, I work shorter hours, take a day off with no pang of conscience (or, at least, not much!), and when one role ends, I have only a few thoughts of replacing it with another. I am fortunate that I have enough money to retire if I wanted (I choose to work, and I am writing this because I want to) and also work in an area that will allow me to continue to work.
>
> It is true that I sometimes miss out on things because I have an appointment that day. It is also true that I sometimes ask myself why I am doing certain things that are not giving me a lot of joy. But, measured in the whole, whether money is important or not, I reckon the benefits of work largely outweigh the frustrations.

CHAPTER 6
The House

Your house is probably your biggest asset — it is for most people. As such, you may think it should deserve a place at the front of this book, but here it is buried at the back of the first part. It is here at the back because most people in retirement think of it as an emergency asset — a back-up if something goes wrong or the money is running out, a back-up in the sense that it is there and available to be used late in retirement if you need some emergency funds.

This is so even though many people now use the house for income, and, often enough, have long planned to do so. Given that your house is probably your biggest asset this seems to me an intelligent approach and there seems no good reason for people to deny themselves the capital that they have in it. Perhaps tapping the house for income should be quite high up in your plans (and further forward in this book!)

Given the house prices that we have today, you probably have a lot of money tied up in your house. This begs two questions:
1. Is it the right amount of house; a Goldilocks-amount house, not too big or too small?
2. How can you use the house both to live in and derive income from?

This chapter looks at both of these questions. They seem simple but, because there are emotional issues tied up in the house, they are quite difficult for many to face. It may be easy to say 'home equity release', 'downsize' or 'take in a boarder' but there are a good number of things to be considered and agreed. There are also a number of things to be done (sale of house, purchase of a house, shifting, finding a tenant/boarder/flatmate, etc.) before any additional money goes into your bank account. Tapping into that major asset (the house) is easier in principal than it is in practice.

Is it the right amount of house?

This question needs to be considered first, preferably in the planning for retirement process rather than when you are living in retirement. There are some people with relatively low-value houses who cannot unlock any meaningful capital by downsizing. At the time of writing, the average price of a Christchurch house is $600,000. Many people from outside of Christchurch have moved there from places with higher house prices and banked significant funds from the move (there are a good number of refugees from Queenstown, which has the highest house prices, averaging $1.15 million). I have seen reports that 30% of Christchurch house sales have been to people from out of town. Some will be property investors and speculators, but many will be downsizing baby boomers.

However, although this may work for people living outside Christchurch, if you live in Christchurch and own an average house, it is hard to downsize. Certainly, you could sell your $600,000 house., but it is hard to buy much in Christchurch for under $500,000. By the time you have paid real estate agents, lawyers, movers, etc., the amount of capital freed up may be hardly worthwhile.

Therefore, you need to think about this early on, to see if downsizing is practicable for you. If not, you need to move on and think about other ways of unlocking capital. If it is practicable and you decide to do it, you should do it well before retirement. This for two reasons:

1. If you have assessed the market you are selling in and the market you are buying into and find that there is a good gap, there is a risk that this gap could close. Perhaps one city saw its property market shift in relation to another and the value gap you were relying on to fund a decent retirement closes. Also, certain types of property may move in value. For example, I have noticed three-bedroom, two-bathroom houses and units have become popular over the last couple of years as baby boomers have retired and downsized in ever-increasing numbers. Executing a downsize strategy is best done sooner rather than later to take advantage of the opportunity that exists in case it changes.
2. It is good to get installed in your new property early in retirement to figure out how things work in the house, to make friends in the area, and to make the house just as you would want. Familiarity in a house is important and, especially if you are moving towns, it is better to do this at the younger end of retirement.

House vs investment?

When you look at your net worth statement, one big asset probably sticks out: there is the house, and then there is the rest. When you really boil things down, you will have a house and an amount that you can put to investment for income. You may have other assets, but I usually ignore most of these unless they are likely to be sold and put to investment — things like cars, boats and other toys are going to be owned throughout most of retirement and, by the time that you come to sell them, they may be worth very little. Sometimes I have seen people with holiday homes that they will sell later in retirement, and I do count these if the proceeds from an eventual sale are going to be put into investments.

For most people, net worth and the things that will make or break retirement come down to the house and money to invest.

Where you draw the line between your house and your investment capital is completely up to you — you have the house and you have investment capital, which will effectively fund your lifestyle. You can choose where you draw the line between them and so set the proportions in each. Unfortunately, perhaps, there is no rule of thumb regarding the proportions for your house and investment — no guide to help you set the 'right' percentages of wealth. This is completely up to you and the way that you want to live in retirement.

House and lifestyle

The amount you have in a house versus the amount of investment capital comes down to the lifestyle you want, how you want to live, and the things that are important to you.

There is a basic conflict between the house and the amount of income that you will have: for every $100,000 that you have in the house, which could go to investments if you downsized, you could have income of either $4,000 p.a. or $6,000 p.a., depending on whether you are going to use 4% or 6% as your drawdown rate. A couple who move from a $1.2 million house (in Auckland) to a $700,000 house (in Christchurch) can put an additional $500,000 to investment. At a 4% drawdown rate this gives an additional $20,000 p.a. of income; at a 6% drawdown they could have an additional $30,000 p.a. income.

Given these kinds of numbers, you have an important choice between the house and the additional income. To make the choice, you need to consider what is important to you — a nice house or the things that you could do with the additional income.

For some people, this choice seems easy: they could travel or, in some way, live very well on the additional income. However, for others, the house is their lifestyle; whether it is the garden, the location, proximity to family/friends or amenities, the view, etc., the house is an important part of the way they live, and this makes for no easy decision.

Asset rich, cash poor is a choice

I frequently hear of people complaining of not being able to do things when they are living in expensive houses. They say, often with a rueful smile, that they are asset rich and cash poor, as if that was somehow imposed on them.

In fact, being asset rich and cash poor is a choice — you could downsize the house and draw a different line between your house and your investments. That is your choice.

Here is a real-life example of a client from some years ago, and although some details are changed for privacy reasons, the numbers are correct. My client was in her early seventies and was recently widowed. We had a planning session in her magnificent house in Remuera and she spent most of the first couple of hours telling me that how she could not afford to visit her daughter and (more importantly) the grandchildren in Paris.

Eventually, I told the client (possibly a little too forcefully) that she could go to Paris as often as she wanted; she just could not make these visits while she lived in this house. She had a choice: the house or family in Paris.

A few months later she sold the house. She achieved $3 million for the house, bought a very nice townhouse for $2 million and so freed up $1 million. With those numbers, Paris was going to be easy.

It seems a very easy decision to make at first blush, but it wasn't: my client had owned the house for over 30 years, she loved it, her children had grown up in it and her husband had died in it. From an intellectual point of view, the decision to downsize was easy; from an emotional point of view, it was not. I have a suspicion that my client knew that I was going to suggest the sale of her house (it was fairly obvious, and most people would quickly see what was needed). In some respects, she was looking for permission from me to sell — she wanted the view of an outsider that it was the right thing to do despite all of her feelings and emotions which suggested the contrary.

The important point is that house prices are extreme in New Zealand — as a country we have bid prices up to very high levels. That gives an opportunity to free up capital (whether downsizing or home equity release) and to live better in retirement. You cannot complain about having only the house — that is usually a choice, and many people can remedy it with the sale of one and the purchase of another.

Two sides of downsizing

Downsizing is not necessarily about the size of the house; it has really come to mean going from a relatively expensive house to a cheaper one (even though the new house may not be smaller). As such, it is mostly about changing the make-up of your net worth so that you have a smaller proportion in your house. When people used to talk about downsizing, they were often meaning having a smaller house when the children had gone; now it usually means downsizing the amount of money you have tied up in housing.

There are two main approaches that should lead to successful downsizing:

1. Moving to a cheaper area. This may mean moving to another city or it may mean moving to another suburb within your city. The point of this is that the location will be regarded as less desirable (i.e. cheaper). Of course, the house itself may be just as desirable but the location may be further from the CBD or more difficult for travel for people who are working. In effect, whether you move to a new town or to a new suburb, you are effectively moving somewhere that most people would find less convenient or less attractive for whatever reason even though you, because you are retired,

find it just fine. As a retired person who no longer needs to commute, the disadvantages that other people who are not retired count as important are not relevant to you. This difference between what retired people value as opposed to younger people lets you unlock capital.
2. Moving to a smaller or older house (or one with fewer amenities). Instead of swapping location (the land), you are swapping the bricks and mortar. This may be preferable for some people because it allows you to stay in the area, close to friends and, possibly, family. However, the house may require more maintenance and it could take time to get used to smaller spaces. Moreover, if you live in a desirable neighbourhood, finding something small and, possibly, a bit run down may not be easy.

There are plenty of people who downsize the actual house and plenty who downsize the location. You need to be careful when downsizing that you unlock enough capital — that will generally come if you are prepared to relocate from suburb or town, but sometimes simply selling a bigger house to buy a smaller house does not unlock much value. This is particularly so when costs to move are taken into account: real estate agents, lawyers, valuers, etc. all cost and there are shifting costs as well. Moreover, I hardly know a soul who has moved into a new house and done nothing with it — people nearly always do something to a new house, even if it is only a coat of paint. You need to think of the capital that you unlock after all costs.

Retirement villages

Retirement villages are being built all over New Zealand at the moment and, on the whole, there is very strong demand. When people look at the value of their homes and compare that to a unit in a retirement village, they see they can effectively downsize and free up some capital. Moreover, many retirement villages are good places to live — generally, you move into a unit that has just been renovated, the villages are quiet and full of people about the same age and with, perhaps, the same interests as you. The units are the ultimate for lock and leave for those who travel a lot and, in many villages, you can move into more care fairly easily when that time comes.

With all of this amenity and freeing up a good amount of cash, what's not to like?

The main thing to understand about a unit in a retirement village is that you do not usually own it. Retirement village documentation varies a great deal but most of them do not offer ownership — instead they sell you a licence to occupy.

As the name suggests, this licence simply gives you the right to live in the unit. Crucially, this means that you do not get the capital gain. In fact, it is worse than this — the amount that you get back on vacating the unit reduces: typically, the value of the licence will reduce as 'deferred management fees' are deducted. These fees could be 30%, which would mean that when you leave the unit, 30% is deducted from the amount that you paid. . This may be calculated on an annual basis for, perhaps, three years at a rate of 10% p.a. to a maximum of 30%. If you leave the unit after one year, you get back the purchase price less 10%, if you leave after two years, the value is reduced by 20%, and after three years or longer, the value that you get back would be 30% less than what you paid.

It is not that you simply get no capital gain — the deduction of 'deferred management fees' mean that you are losing against the price of housing that continues to increase. This means that it is difficult to leave the unit — property is likely to be more expensive and you are going to receive 30% less than what you paid some time ago. To move into a retirement village with this licence to occupy model means you must be very sure that you are there to stay.

I have a friend in Christchurch who, when she was ready to retire, sold her townhouse for $400,000. She purchased a retirement village unit for $350,000. When the Christchurch earthquakes struck, the building was totally destroyed, and she had to move out. She had been in the unit for 10 years, which meant that the maximum deduction was applied (30%) and so she received $245,000 — not enough to buy anything. With the help of friends, she was able to buy another licence in another retirement village but without those friends or other resources, she would have been renting.

The 'deferred management fees' work on an assumption that people only leave their retirement village unit to go into a rest home or to hospital. It is probably quite true that most people do stay long term, but retirement villages which give tenure via a licence to occupy are not something that you should go into unless you are as sure as can be that you will stay. If you end up needing to move on, they certainly reduce options.

There are all sorts of arrangements for retirement villages and many different forms of occupancy. Many retirement villages look like good places to live, however, the licence to occupy seems to be the most common occupancy model, which does feel oppressive for some people — legally they are neither tenants nor owners. The government has announced in 2021 that there will be a review of the legislation by the Retirement Commissioner and many people will watch that with interest.

Downsizing — things to watch

Downsizing is a good thing to do for a lot of people, but it does need to be done early and done once, if possible. Continual shifting is expensive and can be disruptive in terms of trying to establish a place within a community (and your retirement should not become a time of wrangling real estate agents and packing and unpacking if you can avoid it). There are all the usual things that you have to think about when selling your house to buy another one, but there are a few others for people who are thinking about retirement:

1. The property market can move very quickly. If you have decided to do it and all the numbers and other factors work,

you should get on with it. As I write there seems to be a dearth of three-bedroom, two-bathroom houses, which has been put down to the baby boomers buying them up for their retirements.
2. Factor in all the costs. Again, there are the usual ones but remember that you may want to futureproof the house by being able to put in a small lift or have a wet bathroom that has wheelchair access. You may want to do these things while you have the money when you move in.
3. If you downsize to an older house, you may need to bring more maintenance into the budget.
4. There can be social difficulties for those who are moving out of town. It may take more time to build friendships and you may no longer have family support. Mundane things like which electrician to call can also be problems.
5. A smaller, cheaper house may not have the amenities you are used to. Are you sure you will be happy to get rid of a lot of your stuff, and will you be happy with smaller spaces, no view and a whole bunch of new neighbours?
6. It is hard to go back. This is possible for some people but buying and selling houses is an expensive pastime, and one that is not a lot of fun for most of us. Think this through carefully (and do not buy while you are on holiday!).

Staying put and unlocking income

As I said at the beginning of this chapter, for most people the house is their biggest asset. It does need to be seen as the place that you live in first and foremost, but for many it may also be able to contribute to your income. Broadly speaking, there are two main ways you might unlock income from the house: rent out a room or take out a reverse mortgage.

Rent a room

This could involve several different things:
- take in a boarder
- rent a room on short-term rental (Airbnb and the likes)
- put a sleep-out/cabin on the section
- rent the house short term while you move out (perhaps to go camping)

What you might do with the house will depend on the configuration of the house and its size, but also how you want to live your life and the amount of privacy you are prepared to forgo. There are choices in terms of doing short-term or long-term rental, as well as house swaps.

For those who have tight budgets, consideration of some form of renting the house (or a part of the house) is well worth thinking about. Put every idea that is practicable on the table and then give the one that fits with your lifestyle best a go.

Borrowing on the house — Reverse Mortgages

To those who have spent a lifetime getting rid of debt, remortgaging the house cuts against the grain. However, while it would not be my first means of obtaining cash or income, I do think it is a very useful and practical backstop for those who think they are running out of money in retirement.

At the time of writing, there are three companies that provide reverse mortgages — Heartland Bank, SBS Bank, and First Mortgage Trust. Others have offered these products at times, and it is a market that, while small compared to mortgages given to purchase a house, is likely to get bigger and have more providers.

A reverse mortgage is like an ordinary mortgage except you do not pay the interest immediately. Instead it accumulates and is paid back when the house is sold. The provider (the bank) takes mortgage security over your house and advances (lends) you an amount of cash or in some cases gives a monthly income. Interest accrues on the loan, but is not paid until you (or, quite commonly, your estate) sell the house. On the sale of the house, the capital (the amount loaned) and all of the accrued interest are taken by the provider. The interest rate that is charged is higher than ordinary mortgages (perhaps 6% compared to an ordinary mortgage of 2.5%, at the time of writing). This higher rate reflects the fact that interest is not paid in cash but is added to the loan — the provider may not see any cash for some years or even decades. For example, if your house was valued at $500,000 and you wanted to take out 20% in the form of a reverse mortgage, the provider would advance you $100,000. Interest would be charged at say 6% p.a. ($6,000 p.a.) In 20 years' time when the house is sold, the bank takes back the original $100,000 plus the accumulated and compounded interest of $220,000.

In this way, reverse mortgages really are a way to access capital that is otherwise locked up in your house. You have a valuable house, and a reverse mortgage gives you access to cash. You must remember that each time you draw some cash, any inheritance that you were planning to leave reduces further. Moreover, even if you only draw cash once, the amount that you owe will continue to increase as interest accumulates.

You may hope that the house will continue to grow in value and, like anyone who borrows on a house, this capital growth will be yours. It is conceivable that the capital growth of the house will be greater than the interest that is accruing. However, high capital gains cannot be relied upon, whereas you can be absolutely certain that the interest that you have agreed with the provider will be added. Interest ticks away, continuing to mount whatever the circumstances.

This may not bother you — provided that this is certainly your last house, and you are not too worried about the size of inheritances. Difficulties can arise if someone later in retirement wants to sell up and buy another smaller/cheaper home. Depending on what interest has accumulated, this can be difficult.

Most people use reverse mortgages for things like travel, debt consolidation, medical/surgical costs, or repairs to the house. Generally, you are better to use other resources if possible, and that might mean that you draw on savings and investments: the relatively high interest rates that are charged for reverse mortgages mean that you are better to use other resources, which should be less costly for you (or the beneficiaries of your will).

Reverse mortgages can be taken for certain amounts depending on your age. For example, a 65-year-old may be able to borrow 20% of the value of the home, while an 85-year-old may be able to borrow 40%. This amount may vary according to where you live. There are fees to pay at the start and there may also be fees for further loans that you get in the future.

It is important that you check that the reverse mortgage provider has a 'no negative equity' pledge. This is a promise that regardless of how long you live, the interest that is charged or what happens to the value of the house, you will not end up in a situation where you have negative equity, and, on sale, the bank can sue to make up the deficit. Some decades ago, this happened in the UK at times, much to the consternation of the homeowners. Your lawyer should check there is a clause in the loan documents which assures you that this will not happen.

I have often seen people investigate reverse mortgages and discuss it with the children only to find that one of the children is willing and has the capacity to step in and take the bank's role and fund their parents (a direct reversal of the 'bank of mum and dad', which is now so common for the purchase of a first home). This seems to me a good outcome provided that the arrangement is properly documented, and all family members are aware of what is happening.

Some reverse mortgage providers insist that family is involved in their parents' decision to use a reverse mortgage, and also that there is good and proper professional advice (especially legal).

Some retirees regard their house and ability to mortgage it as the back-up for their retirement plans. There is very little evidence that you can take your house with you when you die and, provided you are not too concerned about leaving inheritances, I think that reverse mortgages are a good option for a lot of people.

I reckon #7 — Avoid Selling the house and renting if you can
There are some retirees who would probably be better off (in terms of lifestyle), if they sold their house and rented instead. The sale of the house would give a significant amount of capital and drawing down from this capital would in most cases cover the rent with some left over.

For example, a couple with an average house ($900,000) could sell the house and rent a nice two-bedroom apartment for $700 per week ($36,400 p.a.). If they invested the proceeds from the house sale well and applied a drawdown rate of 5%, they would have $45,000 from their capital, which would mean they were nearly $9,000 p.a. better off. Moreover, they would not have the costs to maintain their house (rates, insurance, maintenance). Financially, they would be better off.

Over and above the Kiwi urge for ownership, there are three problems with the strategy:

1. The drawdown rate or 5% would mean that you were exposed to more longevity risk — that is, you might outlive your savings and end up unable to afford housing of any sort.
2. Inflation (and rents) could rise sharply. Although a properly diversified portfolio ought to cover inflation in part, high inflation would probably make for a very uncomfortable time.
3. There is little or no security of tenure in New Zealand. You would probably end up have to shift fairly often, a pain for anyone but especially those who are trying to enjoy a peaceful, hassle-free retirement.

All in all, although the numbers do make renting in retirement look attractive, it is probably not a good idea unless you are well into retirement. Instead, we need to use a reverse mortgage or one of the other products that are currently being developed to unlock capital in the house.

SECTION 2 —
How to invest in retirement

(Spoiler alert: it's very different from investing pre-retirement.)

CHAPTER 7
The Science of Investing in Retirement

Come retirement, investment is an important business. Most people have at least some money to invest and, no matter whether this is a lot or a little, the science of investment is critical. Even a relatively small amount to invest, one which can only ever give a little supplement to NZ Super, can make a very big difference to the lifestyle you will have in retirement. Moreover, investment is not simply the additional amount of income that you might have, it also involves keeping the money safe.

One of the big decisions to make concerns who will manage your investments. Over the last 30 years I have watched as the investment world has become ever more technical; new investment options have opened up, and tax has become more complicated. It has got harder to keep up with all of this change and, for most of us, the response should be to focus on the basics, and/or to have your investments managed for you, either via a financial adviser or through managed funds. For many years, I encouraged people to look after their own investments but, as markets have changed and expanded, I now think that most people are better off paying fees and having their money managed by a professional.

Given that investment now has many options and has become very complex, few people should take a DIY approach. The investment capital that you have, whether a lot or a little, is now your key asset for a good retirement and it has to be managed well.

Whether you invest through a managed fund or with a financial adviser will largely be dictated by how much money you have to invest; many financial advisers require their clients to have significant amounts of capital, and if you do not meet their minimum threshold, you will need to look at managed funds. As discussed in this section, there are some excellent managed funds available, so investment performance will not necessarily be greatly affected.

A diversified portfolio of some sort or other is critical for those in retirement, regardless of the amount of money that you have. Though it is true that those with more money find it easier to get good investment advice, even those with quite small amounts can use managed funds (often KiwiSaver funds) to give them exposure to all asset classes and diversification within those asset classes.

Most people will no longer want or be able to live off the income from their investments. Interest rates are now too low to derive any meaningful amount of income (especially after the interest income has been taxed and inflation allowed for). Dividends are now also low as share prices have been bid up, and, in any event, many excellent companies that you would want to invest in do not pay dividends.

Instead of this old way of investing in retirement, which involved living off income, retirees need to invest as well as they can and make a steady, regular drawing from a portfolio as set out earlier in this book.

Retirement is now for a long time: the average woman who retires at age 65 can expect to live nearly 25 years in retirement. Over that time (a generation, no less), politics, nature, economies and the markets will throw all sorts of events at you. As an investor, your job is to set yourself up so that you can survive and even thrive during the bad times that will undoubtedly arise.

Asset allocation

Assuming that you are going to have exposure to all the main asset classes (shares, property, fixed interest and cash) you will need to figure out what proportion you will have of each. This is asset allocation, which is simply the percentage of each of the main asset classes that you have in a portfolio or fund.

This is the most critical decision that you will make for your investments (more than anything, it will dictate the returns that you get and the volatility that you will experience). Therefore, the first thing that any investor should do is establish the kind of investor they are and the asset allocation they should have. The main asset classes are growth and income.

Growth assets:
- shares (a.k.a. equities)
- listed property

Income assets:
- fixed interest (a.k.a. bonds)
- cash

Asset allocation is the percentage of each of these that we allocate to a fund and, to make things a bit simpler, we have descriptive terms for the funds or portfolios according to their asset allocation.

A **Conservative fund** would have an asset allocation like this:
- shares 25%
- listed property 5%
- fixed interest 55%
- cash 15%

This portfolio or fund would be said to have 30% in riskier growth assets (shares and listed property) and 70% in less risky income assets (fixed interest and cash).

A **Balanced portfolio** would look like this:
- shares 40%
- listed property 10%

- fixed interest 40%
- cash 10%

This is split 50/50 between growth and income assets.

A **Growth portfolio** would be:
- shares 60%
- listed property 10%
- fixed interest 25%
- cash 5%

This is split 70/30 between growth and income assets.

The above examples split both growth assets and income assets into two: into shares and listed property for growth assets, and fixed interest and cash for income assets. Each of these four main asset classes (shares, listed property, fixed interest and cash) can be split further. For example, shares can be split into international shares, New Zealand shares, emerging markets shares, etc. Fixed interest could be split into international fixed interest, New Zealand fixed interest, emerging markets fixed interest.

There is more on how the various assets are split down further in chapter 8.

Although further splits into many more minor asset classes are common, the really big split to watch out for is between growth and income assets. You will commonly hear talk of a 30/70 portfolio or a 70/30 portfolio and it is this split that is most telling when it comes to risk and return.

Asset allocation is important — numerous studies have shown that the proportion you have of growth assets and income assets will dictate your investment performance (the returns that you get and the volatility risk you will experience) more than anything else. We could spend all of next week arguing about whether you should own shares in Contact Energy or Meridian Energy in a portfolio, but that is unlikely to make any real difference to a portfolio compared to your asset allocation.

Target and tactics

You should note that the examples given above are the target asset allocation — they represent how a fund or portfolio should be invested most of the time. However, a good active fund manager or investor will change the asset allocation to some degree according to the way they see the prospects for the economy and markets and their view of what is likely to happen. These small changes are designed to pick up a bit more return and reduce some risk and are called Tactical Asset Allocation.

For example, your fund manager (if you are investing through a managed fund) may decide that shares look very highly valued, and the sharemarket is heading for a fall. If they have high convictions regarding this, the fund manager could reduce the number of shares the fund owns: a balanced fund, might reduce the number of shares in the portfolio from 40% down to 35% (or less) and put the proceeds from the sale of shares into cash. Hopefully, if the manager proved to be right, when the market has taken its tumble, they could buy the shares back at a cheaper price.

These kinds of tactics (shifting the weight from one asset class to another according to how you see the market) can result in significantly better returns and/or reduced risk. However, making tactical moves ahead of the market is not easy — you are effectively making predictions. And, of course, it can backfire: being worried about a future fall in share prices, you may reduce the number of shares you have only to find the market sail on ever higher! This is a sword with two edges.

Risk — temporary, not permanent

When most people think of investment risk, they think of the likelihood of an investment crashing and burning and the loss of their money. This is thought of as a permanent loss — one where they are not going to see their money again.

Portfolio investors, people who invest in all of the asset classes and are diversified within each asset class, do not think of risk like this. Portfolio investors are invested in dozens (or hundreds and sometimes thousands) of different investments, and they know that they are not all going to crash and burn.

Instead, portfolio investors think of risk as volatility — the ups and downs investors are going to have to tolerate while they get their expected return. Investment professionals can calculate the returns that you would expect to get from a particular portfolio, and then calculate the amount of volatility an investor with that portfolio would experience. In this respect, investment becomes quite mathematical — statistics are used to calculate likelihoods and probabilities.

The important thing for a retired investor to know is that the risk of a diversified portfolio is much more about temporary ups and downs (volatility) rather than absolute loss. If all of these companies that you have invested in go broke, the world is in so much trouble that you probably have worries greater than what is happening to your money. Instead, with a diversified portfolio, you will expect to suffer volatility. This volatility is uncomfortable but not as uncomfortable as ownership of just one or two investments that might have absolute loss.

You have to take risk — but the right amount of risk

Investors get paid to take risk and investment starts by looking at risk. We all want to get good returns but, first and foremost, we need to think about the amount of risk that we can tolerate.

To get an investment return you have to take some sort of risk, however we are all different when it comes to the amount of risk we can tolerate. You may remember the couple at the start of this book who woke up to find $7,595,777 in their bank account and whose main emotion was fear. I helped this couple survey all of their investment options and they quite quickly realised that there was nothing they could do with this money that is riskless. Even leaving it in the bank scared them — that was one of the safest things that they could do with their money but, even so, they knew that banks do sometimes fail and, in any event, after tax and an allowance for inflation, they knew that leaving it in the bank would mean that they were losing their purchasing power.

The investor's job is not to get rid of risk (you can't). Instead, it is to take the right amount of risk (an amount you can tolerate) by getting the right proportion in each asset class: the right amount of shares and property, and the right amount of fixed interest and cash.

You can then mitigate the risk that you are taking by diversifying within each asset class. Portfolio investors do not suffer absolute loss, but the more shares they have in a portfolio, the greater the volatility they will experience.

Of course, the greater the volatility you can tolerate, the greater the returns you should expect. The Financial Markets Authority gives expected returns for portfolios at each level of risk:

- conservative 2.5% p.a.
- balanced 3.5% p.a.
- growth 4.5% p.a.

These are the expected returns after fees and after tax at 28%. If you look at returns from KiwiSaver since its beginnings in 2007, you see very clearly that funds with more shares got greater returns, but they came with higher volatility risk. Over time, the theory of greater risk leading to greater returns works near perfectly in practice!

Asset allocation for retired folk

Although there is no hard and fast rule, most retirees should invest in either a conservative fund (30/70) or a balanced fund (50/50). Certainly, very few retired people should be invested more aggressively than this with a greater number of shares and the greater volatility risk that comes with it. While as a matter of tactics they may be more aggressively invested for a while so that they can take advantage of some event, this should not be a long-term position and they should go back to their correct asset allocation fairly quickly.

Retirees need to be very careful with their asset allocation and, in particular, the amount of shares they have in their portfolios. A major market downturn leaves someone with a lot of shares vulnerable. Beware, too, investing tactically in more shares for a short time as downturns can come quite unexpectedly as events occur (think of 9/11 or other geopolitical events). Even though these kinds of events may be relatively short term (i.e. they correct within a few months and the market goes back to where it was fairly soon), they can have long lasting effects on your financial position:

1. Remember that you are drawing down on the portfolio regularly. When you draw down you don't simply draw returns but part of the capital as well — you will be selling some of your investments and selling during a slump is most disadvantageous. Selling when the markets are down makes your loss permanent because you no longer own the assets, which, having fallen, will one day rebound and would have got you your money back.

2. While most market slumps last a few months (perhaps a year or two), there are some downturns through history which have lasted years and even decades (e.g. the 1929 crash in the US, and the 1989 sharemarket fall in Japan, which 32 years later has still not recovered its original value). You do not want to be caught with too much invested in shares during these kinds of events.

3. Major downturns frighten some people into selling. We all know that we are meant to buy in gloom and sell in boom, but many people do precisely the opposite. Over my career I have seen many people get rattled out of the market permanently, frightened by a market downturn and the inevitable

accompanying wall of negative noise that comes out of the media at these times. Selling in a slump turns temporary volatility (which is uncomfortable) into permanent losses.

Therefore, choose your asset allocation carefully and consider risk before you consider return. In effect, investors need to consider the amount of volatility they can tolerate financially and the amount they are comfortable with personally. The key thing with retirees is that they are drawing on capital steadily and, therefore, cannot tolerate periods when the value of their portfolios are down for too long, nor down too far. A balanced portfolio would likely be the upper limit of risk for nearly all.

If you do decide to make a tactical move, try not to stay away from your targeted asset allocation for too long (especially if you are loading up on shares). Making tactical investment moves can be a risky game — you may be right regarding the market being over-valued (or under-valued) but it may be that the market may not agree with your assessment. It may be a long wait before anything moves in your favour and, to paraphrase John Maynard Keynes, the market may be wrong for longer than you can stay solvent. There are many people who do not make tactical moves but simply sit through all events holding on to their target asset allocation and, unless you think you are especially well informed, you should consider being one of them.

There are some people who may want to be between balanced and conservative portfolios. This can be managed quite easily by those who manage their own money or have a bespoke portfolio with a financial adviser. Those who want investment exposures that are between conservative and balanced and who are investing through managed funds can consider having half of their money in a conservative fund and the other half in a balanced one. As I write, I have some of my money invested like this: half of my KiwiSaver money is with the provider's balanced fund and the other half with the conservative. Overall, this would give me roughly 40% exposure to shares and listed property, and 60% to fixed interest and cash. I have other funds that are more aggressively invested but, of course, I am not retired yet.

Selecting your asset allocation — conservative, balanced or growth

This is the first — and most important — thing that any investor can do. Establishing your correct asset allocation is likely to be the thing that keeps your investments safe more than any other single thing (being diversified within each asset class comes second).

Most people will probably not set their asset allocation, as such, but will instead establish the kind of investor they should be — i.e. conservative, balanced or aggressive. These are simply the shorthand names that are given to the asset allocations as shown above. Generally, if you did an online questionnaire (often called a risk finder, risk tolerance calculator, risk profiler, etc.), you will not get the proportions of each asset class but instead a name which describes the sort of portfolio you should have.

There is sometimes confusion regarding these names. It is important to know that these do not describe you as a person — just because you come out as an aggressive investor does not mean that that you stomp around the place, shake your fists, and bare your teeth whenever you get a bit cross. Instead, they are descriptions of the kind of portfolio that should be useful for you: i.e. if you have come out as conservative, you should find a fund that is 30% invested in growth assets, 70% in income assets (or, if you are investing yourself, you should build a portfolio that sticks to the same kind of income/growth split).

I would encourage everyone to regularly do one or more of these questionnaires — there are plenty available online, including one at www.sorted.org.nz. It may pay to do more than one, especially if the first one that you do is suggesting a level of risk that does not seem appropriate for you — these questionnaires are free and take little more than a couple of minutes; do a few of them if you need to.

If you are a couple, you should both do risk questionnaires. In the event that you come out with a different risk profile than your partner, it would pay to adopt the one that is most risk averse. While getting lower returns may be a little frustrating for one partner, it is better than dragging the other partner into a situation where he or she has to take risk beyond comfort. A little frustration with lower returns is a lot better than sleepless nights worrying about investment risk, which could lead through to selling investments in the bottom of a slump.

What drives risk tolerance

There is an old rule of thumb that says you should have a percentage of growth assets (shares and listed property) that is equivalent to 100 less your age. This would mean that 20-year-olds would have 80% of their portfolio in shares and listed property (100 - 20 = 80) but that a 60-year-old would have 40% in shares and property (100 - 60 = 40).

Like all rules of thumb, this is a bit rough and ready. My main criticism of it would be that it only takes into account time as a factor and, as you will see, there are two other factors that are important in deciding how much risk you can take. Time is an important factor, but it is by no means the only one.

When you do a questionnaire for your risk tolerance, there are three main factors that will dictate the amount of risk you should take. Depending on how you answer the questions, each factor will suggest that you take on more or less risk.

Time factor

This factor considers and asks about the length of time you will be investing for. The longer the time until you need your money back, the greater the chance for risky, volatile assets (like shares) to give you higher returns; but if you are investing for a short time, there is a reasonable chance that markets will be down at just the time when you want your money back. I can say with reasonable confidence that if you invested in a share fund and kept your money in it for 30 years, you would get an investment return of about 10% (with a lot of ups and downs). However, if you invested in the same fund and planned to take your money out the next day, I would have no idea what your returns might be (that single day could prove to be very good or very poor).

This is a tricky one for retired investors: they may remain invested in their portfolio for 25 years or more but, as they are drawing down on their portfolios on a fortnightly basis, they are effectively making a whole lot of little withdrawals as they go through retirement. This is not like someone who is saving to buy a car and who expects to withdraw their money in one year; nor is it like someone saving for retirement in 30 years. Both of these have one final drawdown day whereas retired investors have many over the course of retirement.

This makes the time factor neutral for retired investors — they are not investing for the very long term, but neither are they short-term investors. Nevertheless, it has always seemed to me that as time goes by within retirement, you should, as the rule of thumb 100 less your age suggests, reduce risk by reducing the amount that you have in shares and property. Rather than doing this every year, as this rule of thumb suggests, I think that most people should start retirement by investing in a balanced portfolio (subject to the other two factors below) but as they age, lower the risk. Quite simply, for most people this suggests that the 65-year-old who starts off with a balanced portfolio might, by age 80 or 85, have moved to a conservative one.

Financial capacity

This factor should consider your overall financial circumstances and your ability to cope with a significant economic or market shock. You need to think about what happens to your financial position and to your life in retirement, if (when) there is another GFC-like event with all of its market turmoil. The key question is: if economies around the world are in turmoil, banks are failing and markets are in freefall, how well will you be able to cope?

Retired people are at least partially dependent on the performance of their investment portfolios for their incomes and their lives. Kiwis are fortunate that we all have NZ Super which can provide the basics of life, and that is likely to be paid in just about any circumstances. Beyond NZ Super is perhaps some work, and/or some income from renting a room in the house.

Investments, and drawing from a portfolio, fill a gap and for many provide spice to life beyond the basics. While a few wealthy people will have plenty of ability to withstand a major economic or market shock, most people depend on drawing from their portfolios to maintain their lifestyle (although if you have a 'lake of cash' as outlined on page 64, you are better equipped to withstand slumps).

Most retired people cannot tolerate the extreme volatility of a major market crash when their portfolio is biased most heavily to volatile assets. The low capacity to withstand volatility and the fact that virtually all retired people need to draw on their savings are together the reason, I believe, that few retired people should be invested with a 50/50 portfolio. Investing more aggressively in shares is not wise in retirement.

There is an exception to this: those who are so wealthy they are unlikely to use all of their investment capital. These people expect to leave large inheritances to future generations and, as such, are effectively investing for the children. They can afford to take the additional risk and, one day, the children may be glad that they did.

Remember that you will probably be dependent on your portfolio or fund for your income; this is not like a 40-year-old doctor who has nearly paid off the mortgage and is never likely to be without work. This person has plenty of financial capacity and has the capacity to withstand recessions and slumps easily. A retired person is in no such situation and ought to take lower risk.

Psychological factors

This is your mental or emotional make-up and concerns how you feel when markets are down and your portfolio much reduced in value. This is not just about feelings — it also concerns what you will do when there is a major slump. Feeling sick or scared when there is volatility is not good, selling out at the bottom of a slump is even worse.

If you have never experienced a major slump in the value of your savings, it can be difficult to judge how you will feel and what you will do when your investments are worth less than you thought. Remember that economic difficulties and market slumps do not happen in a vacuum — you do not just get up one morning, have a look at your portfolio and see that the value is 20% less than what it was when you last looked. Market slumps happen to the noise of an excited news media; there is a wall of noise coming from market commentators and, when you experience this noise, you would be forgiven if you believed the world was going to end about 3.30 this afternoon. For younger people, who know they have time for things to right themselves again, standing up against this wall of negative noise is relatively easy; for an older person, who has less time and who is drawing funds out of the portfolio every fortnight, a retreat back to the safety of bank deposits could seem a very good idea (even though it usually is not!).

It is difficult to predict how someone who has not experienced market slumps will react. The question I would ask of clients is this: so, you put your $500,000 into the markets today and a week later the portfolio is worth $400,000, how will you feel and what will you do? A fall like this is always possible — even a balanced fund could quickly fall 20%. Try to imagine it — and then think hard about your asset allocation.

This psychological aspect of investment (how you will feel and what you might do) trumps the other three factors. By this I mean that it does not matter how long you are investing for, nor how good your financial capacity, if you are going to be so rattled in a slump that you will sell out at or near the bottom, you should invest more conservatively. Yes, this means lower returns and your money will not last as long, but that is better than selling and taking a permanent loss.

Beware risk creep

When you have set your asset allocation and you are investing, you need to be careful that you do not move too far from the risk levels that you established. It can be very tempting to gradually increase the amount of shares and listed property that you own, especially when the market is doing well. When you are being well rewarded for owning shares it can become almost natural to want to own more of them and so the proportion in shares creeps up.

Market turnarounds can happen overnight (literally, in the case of international shares) and by the time you have realised your mistake, it is too late.

This is less of a problem for those who are investing through managed funds: these funds nearly always stick quite closely to their asset allocation unless they make a conscious decision to make a tactical move. Nevertheless, a good fund manager knows the importance of asset allocation and knows they will have a lot of investors quite grumpy if they make a wrong move. They are, therefore, cautious and usually only make a move after a lot of thought and internal debate. Even then, the increase of one asset class at the expense of another will usually be relatively small.

This should also be the case for those giving their money to financial advisers to invest for them. Usually, they will be quite cautious and not move away from an agreed asset allocation without good cause.

In my experience, it is the DIY investors who need to be most cautious of risk creep. They have always seemed most likely to keep on buying shares which are doing well for them — I have several times seen DIY investors who have ended up with portfolios almost completely made up of shares, with little or nothing in fixed interest or cash. When a slump comes, these people are badly affected.

Selling in a market slump — the worst case scenario

The worst thing that can happen to any investor is they become a forced seller at the time of a market slump. By selling, they come out of the market and the loss becomes permanent rather than just volatility. Selling in a slump usually happens for one ot two reasons:

1. Investors have taken on more risk than they can tolerate. These people are rattled out of the market and, frequently, will not go back in for love nor money.
2. People get a need for some money during the slump. This withdrawal may have been planned, e.g. a lot of people were found to be saving for their first house purchase in KiwiSaver accounts that were too aggressive during the first wave of COVID. These people either wanted to buy soon (and so withdrew their money) or felt very uncomfortable that their balance was down 20% or more (and so withdrew their money).

Retired people are making regular withdrawals and so are making small sales of shares during slumps. To avoid this, one of the best things you can do is hold an amount of cash outside the portfolio, which can be used while the market is down as outlined on page 64.

A thought experiment (Japan)

I have said that most market slumps last only a few months or, perhaps, a couple of years. At the time I noted that the US crash of 1929 was an exception as was the Japanese crash of 1989. A little more detail on Japan in 1989 might be instructional.

In December 1989, the main Japanese share index (the Nikkei

225) peaked at 39,915. It fell from there and kept on falling through to March 2003 when it reached 7862 (losing about 80% of its value). From 39,915 to 7862 over a period of 14 years is one very big crash. Worse, perhaps for those heavily exposed to shares and still holding on grimly, the Japanese market today has still not recovered: at 27,396 and 32 years later, Japanese shares are still over 30% below their peak.

There are exceptions to the fairly quick recovery rule — sometimes it would have been better to have sold out. However, although the general rule still holds for my money, these exceptions like Japan in 1989 and the US in 1929 should sober up anyone who is thinking of having everything (or anything close to everything) in shares.

Final word on risk

Warren Buffett has something to say about people who get a bit carried away with themselves and who take on too much risk. Buffett said: it is only when the tide goes out that we discover who has been swimming naked.

That hardly needs any explanation — as always Buffett puts it succinctly and his pithy little saying goes straight to the heart of the matter.

It is when the tide is in that we need to be sure that our togs are on. When markets run strongly, and returns are high we tend to fall into a trap, which is that we think we (or our advisers or fund managers) are wonderful investors and can do no wrong. This hubris is most dangerous: we get full of ourselves and think that the tide is in permanently. It is not and soon enough you will find yourself exposed and worse than embarrassed.

Having said all of this, I am not making a case for retirees to shun risk. You need to take risk; nothing ever happens unless you take a risk and you will get no return without risk.

Just make sure it is the right amount of risk.

> **I reckon #8 — Planning is key**
>
> In retirement, you play the investment game for keeps. It is the setup, the planning that you will do in the lead-up to retirement, that is important. The key areas are covered in this book, but these three things are so critical that they warrant summary here:
>
> 1. Do a few of the multitude of 'risk finder' questionnaires that are available online so that you are certain you have your asset allocation correct.
>
> 2. Have a 'lake of cash' outside the portfolio — an amount of liquid money at the bank that you can get at in emergency and/or live on so that you do not have to draw from your fund or portfolio during slumps.
>
> 3. Consider carefully who will manage the money for you — it probably will not be you.

CHAPTER 8
Asset Classes and Risk Management

Typically, a portfolio for people starting off in retirement would have 50% in growth assets and 50% in income, i.e. it would be a balanced portfolio (or a balanced fund). Digging a little deeper it would have a range of asset classes in both the income and growth categories and would look something like this:
New Zealand shares 15%
Australian shares 5%
International shares 25%
Listed property 5%
Total growth assets 50%

New Zealand fixed interest rates 30%
International fixed interest rates 15%
Cash 5%
Total income assets 50%

As you can see, there are four asset classes in the growth category, and three in the income category. There could be more than this if you wanted — for example, under the growth category you could have an allocation to emerging markets shares or an allocation to global infrastructure; under the income category you could have emerging markets fixed interest or some Australian cash. However, the portfolio above covers the main asset classes and there is often little or no point overly complicating the portfolio and having to find investments that fit into other relatively small asset classes. For example, it is probably not worth the effort of finding the right fund so that you can have 2.5% of the portfolio in global infrastructure.

Ultimately, once asset allocation is set, investors need to decide on how they will fill each asset class, i.e. they need to work out which securities they will buy in each investment type to give them the desired exposures. This is called 'investment selection'. Many inexperienced investors get this cart before that horse; they are so enthusiastic to start making investments that they immediately start to consider which investments they will buy (which particular shares, or which funds). However, this is a time to hold your horses; the first thing is to get asset allocation right and then, but only then, start to look at the specific investment that you will have.

A useful way of thinking of this is that you will have several different buckets, one for each different asset class. Only when you know how much you will put in each bucket should you start to consider what you will fill the buckets with.

Seven buckets

To some people, it seems a waste of time and an overcomplication to have seven (and sometimes more!) different asset classes — why, these people ask, do we not just have some New Zealand shares and some New Zealand fixed interest? We could have just these two asset classes in the right proportions so that our risk would be suitable for us — easy and uncomplicated. That would be much simpler than trying to get exposure to seven different asset classes with all the faffing around that comes with it.

Well, you could have just one asset class for both of your growth assets and your income, and, yes, New Zealand shares and New

Zealand fixed interest would probably do the job. And, yes, it would certainly be a much easier portfolio to manage with just the two asset classes.

However, as you will see in a moment, such a two-asset-class portfolio would be quite a blunt instrument. Each of the seven different asset classes that I have listed above gives different performance — both returns and volatility are likely to be different. Having more asset classes than just two gives greater diversification and would be expected to perform differently according to whatever was going on in economies and markets.

Investors look for negative correlations. This is a way of saying they want investments that will perform the opposite of other investments. This means they look for an asset class which will perform well when another is performing badly.

Of course, investors seldom get perfect negative correlations: a perfect negative correlation would be that when investment A falls by 20%, investment B rises by 20%. Unfortunately, that perfect negative correlation rarely happens, but it certainly does happen that some investment types generally move in the opposite way of others.

An asset class for all (economic) seasons

Another way to think of this is that you are looking to have a portfolio that has a range of asset classes so that you will always have at least one that will perform well in any particular expected economic or market event, or climate. If you can cover all the most likely economic events with asset classes that will perform well no matter what event comes to pass, you are a lot safer and more secure than if you simply own two asset classes, i.e. you have less risk. For example, if you have an allocation to some international shares and something happens to the New Zealand economy, you will at least have a part of the portfolio doing well for you.

It is useful to think of each asset class and what it will do for you, and what economic background will make it do well or poorly:

Asset class	Returns	Volatility risk	Provides cover for
NZ shares	High	High	Strong economy, inflation
Australian shares	High	Very high	Strong economy, inflation, NZ-specific event
International shares	High	Extremely high	Strong economy, inflation, NZ-specific event
Listed property	Medium/high	High	Strong economy, inflation
NZ Fixed interest	Medium	Low/medium	Recession, deflation
Global fixed interest	Medium	Low/medium	Recession, deflation, NZ-specific event
Cash	Low	Low	Recession, major market fall

This chart gives an idea of why you need to have each of these seven asset classes. The chart is a little approximate — for example, generally, the volatility of NZ fixed interest is fairly low, but in some circumstances, it can be higher, especially if you buy fixed interest securities with quite low credit ratings.

Some people may think it is strange that we look for asset classes that will cover us if the economy is very strong. I am not really using the word 'cover' in the sense that we think about it as insurance. Instead, I think about the events that can happen (and the economic climates that might prevail) and the asset classes that will do well during those times. You want assets that will do well when the economy is strong and growing, so that you take advantage of the very good returns that are on offer then, just as you need investments that will do relatively well when the economy is poor.

Bad weather is certain

I have seen four major market crashes over my investment life of about 40 years: the 1987 crash, dot-com crash, the GFC and COVID. If you look further back in history, there are plenty of other market crashes from the Dutch tulip bulb bubble and crash in 1637, the South Seas bubble in the 18th century through to the 1929 Wall Street crash. Looking at history, it seems to me that today these market crashes are coming more frequently — this may be simply a matter of the way that the numbers have fallen, but over the course of retirement, you are likely to experience at least one market crash, and quite possibly more. As someone who is dependent on a portfolio for at least part of your income, you should be ready for it (or them). Your first line of defence is the right asset allocation.

On average, you will spend around 25 years in retirement. Some people will have less than that, some people more — a few may have 40 years! Over that sort of time period (multiple decades), there will be all sorts of economic weather: good, bad and indifferent. Some events may seem very big at the time but, in reality, make little different to your investment; others may sneak up slowly and quietly but have profound effects on your investments.

Throughout all the time that you are investing in retirement, you have to keep firmly in mind that there is no single asset class that will do well in all seasons.

There is an investment for whatever might happen; you do not know exactly what is going to happen so you need to own a bit of every investment type.

I have here considered just five common things that may happen to the economy over the course of your retirement. What triggers any of these economic events (geopolitical events, banking crisis, climate change, biosecurity breach, natural disaster, etc.) is neither here nor there: the five things below will be the main outcome of whatever is going on:

- buoyant, strong economy
- recession

- inflation
- deflation
- New Zealand-specific event

These five are the main things investors need to be concerned about, but other economic climates could prevail (e.g. stagflation), triggered by a range of different events: global conflict, pandemic, etc. Of course, you cannot foresee every economic climate and, these things (strong economy, recession, inflation, deflation and New Zealand-specific event) are the most likely outcomes that you need to be ready for.

Let's have a look at the seven asset classes that most people will have in their portfolios and consider what they will do for you, and why you need to have them.

New Zealand shares

There should be some New Zealand shares in nearly all retired people's portfolios. There is a familiarity to the New Zealand market and its companies — investing on home ground is easier than further afield.

New Zealand shares tend to give high returns, higher than the shares from most other places around the world — and these higher New Zealand returns come with no currency risk. You would expect higher returns because New Zealand shares are based on a country with a small and brittle economy, and so we need to be cheaper with higher returns to attract international investors. The New Zealand sharemarket is under researched, so it is relatively easy for fund managers and other skilled investors to outperform the market. A lack of research means that there are likely to be mis-pricings that can be exploited.

New Zealand is also unusual in that around 50% of the shares on the New Zealand market are owned by people from outside New Zealand. These investors are not always looking for every little bit of extra return they can get. They are often not fighting for the last penny but just looking for the exposure. This is one of the main reasons that Mercer (a fund manager, researcher and adviser) has consistently found that in New Zealand, the average fund manager beats the market. Home advantage is important.

However, as noted above, New Zealand's economy is small and brittle — imagine what would happen to the economy here if New Zealand got foot and mouth disease! Moreover, the New Zealand sharemarket is rather limited — while there are some good companies operating in good industries which are listed, there are also some big gaps (big brands, tech, healthcare, artificial intelligence). To invest in most of the big global trends that are happening at the moment, you have to invest outside New Zealand.

What are New Zealand shares good for? New Zealand shares do well when the economy is buoyant, and many companies provide cover against inflation.

Australian shares

Most people invest in the sharemarkets of our nearest neighbour and second biggest trading partner. Australia has indeed been the lucky country and, up until COVID struck, it had not endured a recession for 29 years. It is a country rich in natural resources, although it does have some vulnerabilities as the climate changes.

Australian shares do give you exposure to industries that are mostly unavailable on the New Zealand market: banking and mining in particular. The Australian market gives some diversification and a lot of us are fairly familiar with many of the companies that we often buy into. Like New Zealand, the Australian market is fairly well regulated, and, unlike New Zealand, it does have an active options market.

The downside of the Australian market is that dividends are effectively double taxed — Kiwi investors do not get the franking credits (similar to our imputation credits) meaning that there is no credit for the tax that the companies have already paid. Moreover, the diversification is by no means perfect — Australia and New Zealand are joined at the hip — although we love to poke a stick at our big brother occasionally, in effect, we are very close economically and, under many economic scenarios, where they go, so will we. Finally, there is currency risk when you own Australian shares, and this increases volatility.

What are Australian shares good for? Australian shares will do well when the world economy is buoyant (resources usually do very well at these times) and they do provide some cover for inflation.

International shares

International shares are a must in every portfolio. They cover Kiwi investors for any kind of adverse event that is New Zealand specific (e.g. a major biosecurity breach or some natural disaster). They also give exposure to some of the big trends, industries and brands that dominate the global market, and which have made very large amounts of money (and will probably continue to make very large amounts of money).

I do not think that we can live in a small place like New Zealand and ignore some of the world-change trends that are happening: artificial intelligence, robotics, biotechnology, cleantech, medical devices — it could be a long and important list. The returns from some of these have been stunning (for example, since Amazon's shares listed 24 years ago, the company has given shareholders returns of 37% p.a.) I have often thought that restricting yourself to just New Zealand shares is much the same as living in Cricklewood and restricting yourself to Cricklewood investments.

Moreover, you get the best diversification with international shares — there are plenty of scenarios where Australasia could have economic problems but the rest of the world sails on, doing well. International shares give diversification not just by geography but by industry as well — there are plenty of industries (whether new like tech or older like railways) that you simply cannot buy into in New Zealand.

There are three main difficulties with international shares: first, they are more volatile. Not only do the price of the shares go up and down, but the various currencies (US dollar, Euro, Sterling, Singapore dollar) that you might be investing in also move around. Second, the names of many of the companies and what they do are not familiar. Moreover, it is difficult (although perhaps not impossible) to know which companies will come through in particular industries and be winners — most Kiwi investors should take their international shares exposures through managed funds. Third, international shares are usually taxed differently through the Foreign Investment Funds regime. Although this is not a particularly onerous tax, it is complicated and demands excellent record keeping (which is usually provided by the platform that you are investing through — see page 166).

What are international shares good for? International shares are essential for Kiwi investors and do well when the global economy is buoyant. They also cover Kiwi investors for inflation and for Australasia-specific adverse events.

Listed property

My favourite! I have long thought that if someone changed the rules and we were only allowed to invest in one asset class, it would be commercial property. To get this exposure I would not go out and try to buy buildings but would buy the shares of property-owning companies (hopefully companies that owned property around the world, if the rules allowed for that).

No single asset class gives everything and covers you against all events, and so I do not solely invest in commercial property — but commercial property gives good income from rents, income that grows over time, and capital gain. Listed property is sometimes likened to a hybrid between shares in a company and fixed interest: steady income with some capital and income growth. This is not really true — it is an equity asset and, although the volatility may be a little less than most other shares in companies, it is still significant.

Listed property gives exposure to some of the best commercial property in the country. Its performance is usually correlated to shares but with listed property, the cash flow through dividends is likely to continue (possibly at a lower rate) because of the long leases. As such, although the share price is volatile on the market, I think that commercial property purchased on the sharemarket is less risky than many shares.

What is listed property good for? Listed property performs well in buoyant times and gives cover against inflation.

New Zealand fixed interest (also known as New Zealand bonds)

There was a time when many retirees invested in bank deposits and fixed interest — and not much else. This was a mistake and with the gradual fall in interest rates of the last thirty years (with a major acceleration to that fall at the time of COVID), most have now seen that this is not a valid investment strategy. It never really was terribly good, but because interest rates have generally fallen since the early 1990s, there were people in the previous generation who were lucky enough to have got away with fixed interest as their only strategy.

The returns from fixed interest investments in coming years and decades are likely to be lower than they have been in the past — falling interest rates gave profits over the last 30 years but that is unlikely to continue to the same or any extent in the future. Nevertheless, there is still good reason to have fixed interest in your portfolio: although interest rates are very low, they can go lower still (many countries around the world have lived with negative interest rates over the last decade) and, at times of economic difficulty, interest rates are likely to fall.

The real purpose of fixed interest is that it locks in an interest rate which, although it may seem low at the time, will appear to be very good if interest rates fall. Fixed interest is really some insurance against a fall in interest rates; that fall most likely having been prompted by the prospect of a recession.

When interest rates fall, fixed interest securities become more valuable (i.e. their prices rise) and that is helpful to a portfolio if it is being battered by falling share prices (this fall is probably also being created by that same recession). As such, fixed interest balances the portfolio. Most people buy fixed interest investments for the income, planning to hold them until maturity. Although this is certainly a valid approach, you have to consider the way that fixed interest is often negatively correlated with shares — when share prices go up, fixed interest prices go down, and vice versa.

At the time of writing, fixed interest rates are only around 2% p.a. (give or take according to the duration and credit standing of the issuer). If you tax this at 30%, the tax paid yield comes down to 1.4%. With inflation running at 5% at the time of writing, you are losing money.

However, and here is the dilemma, you cannot have a whole portfolio of shares — it would be too volatile. And so, you have to own some fixed interest, knowing that you are probably taking a loss on it, just to balance the portfolio and to cover the possibility of interest rates falling any further.

What is fixed interest good for? Fixed interest tends to do well as recession looms and strikes. In times of deflation (consumer prices falling) it can do extremely well as interest rates tumble.

Global fixed interest (also known as global bonds)

Global fixed interest is very similar to New Zealand fixed interest. The important thing with global fixed interest (and the reason you will probably invest in it) is that it gives you diversification. Instead of investing in the usual fixed interest securities from companies like Infratil, Sky City, Contact Energy etc., along with the banks and some property companies (some of which you will probably own the shares of), you get to lend your money to some of the biggest and most famous companies around the world. You can also buy fixed interest investments that are issued by governments, which gives exposure to some of the strongest economies in the world. Diversifying away from the usual New Zealand fixed interest issuers has much to recommend it.

However, before you dive into it, understand that there are some other quite important differences:

1. Global fixed interest is almost always invested through managed funds in New Zealand. I know of no one who makes their own direct fixed interest investments into companies and governments around the world — it is probably mostly too hard to hedge the currency (see below).
2. All funds that I know of that are in global fixed interest are hedged back to the New Zealand dollar. This hedging is important because one small movement in the currency could wipe out your entire annual interest payment overnight. Hedging the currency takes out this risk.
3. Most of the global fixed interest funds do not simply buy fixed interest securities and then hold them until maturity. They position the portfolio according to how they see the economic and market situation, trading securities frequently as they try to maximise returns.
4. Some global fixed interest securities are for very long periods of time. While most New Zealand fixed interest has duration of five to eight years, internationally there are plenty of fixed interest securities with 30 years' duration and some are for as long as 100 years.

What is global fixed interest good for? Global fixed interest helps with diversification and is very useful in a portfolio when there is recession or deflation.

Cash

Cash gives lousy returns — it always has and it probably always will. However, it comes with low volatility (VERY low volatility). The really good thing about cash is that your money is there on immediate or, at least, very short notice.

Cash is usually defined as funds that are tied up for less than 90 days (some definitions go out to 180 days and a few talk about one year). This means that a term deposit with 60 days until maturity is regarded as cash, but a term deposit with two years to run is not.

When recessions strike and markets fall, most people are delighted to have some cash (each time I have watched a crash in this country I have seen commentators say that cash is king). Cash has a place in all portfolios because we can never be quite sure when that fall might happen — having some cash in a recession usually means that you can buy some very cheap shares. Also, cash is very valuable to retired people at times of falling sharemarkets because it means that you are able to use these funds to live on without having to sell investments while waiting for markets to recover.

While you should always hold some cash, you do not want to hold too much for too long — the returns are just so poor. Nor ought you adopt a strategy of simply rolling over term deposits and living off the interest. While it is perhaps the safest asset class, like all asset classes, cash has its vulnerabilities:

- Cash is devalued by inflation. After tax, the returns from cash seldom keep up with inflation — holding cash is probably making you poorer by the day.
- Banks do fail. New Zealand is one of the few countries in the world where the government does not guarantee bank deposits. There was a government guarantee during the GFC but that was removed when the crisis was over. There seem to be government plans to introduce a permanent guarantee but at the time of writing this is not settled.

What is cash good for? Cash is a critical asset class for all retirees and is most important during recessions and market falls.

> **I reckon #9 — Keep your portfolio simple**
>
> There are other asset classes that you could choose to invest in: for example, emerging markets shares have been very popular at times, but I reckon it pays to keep a portfolio reasonably stripped down and simple. This is particularly so if you are managing a portfolio yourself — I am not concerned if fund managers or financial advisers build portfolios with more asset classes. Each asset class that you have needs to have individual investments selected for it. If you are managing a portfolio yourself, you probably do not want the additional burden of finding investments in asset classes like emerging markets or global infrastructure.

CHAPTER 9
Investment selection and Getting Help

Once you know how much you should have in each asset class, you need to think about the types of investments that will give you the required exposures. This means you have to think about the investments that you will make, and how you will make them along with what help and advice you will get.

This requires you to make some decisions regarding your investment style and who you will get to advise you. There are many options, but they boil down to four main things:

1. You could use managed funds. You could use managed funds of varying sorts; perhaps have one Multi Asset Class fund which has all the asset classes in it, or build a portfolio of Single Asset Class funds so that you have exposure to all asset classes in the right proportion.
2. You could buy companies directly, i.e. you could have some account with a brokerage house or a platform like Sharesies or Hatch.
3. You could have a combination of both, some managed funds with a few individual companies that you think will really outperform.
4. You could have a managed account through a financial adviser.

Show me the money

The way you invest your money, and who you use to help you build a portfolio with the right asset allocation, will depend on how much you have to invest. That sounds sad but it is true that those with less money have some options closed off. There are many financial advisers who require minimum amounts before they will take on clients: sometimes this minimum is $250,000; some others may apply a minimum of $500,000 and there are a few who would require you to have $1 million before they would advise and manage your money for you.

This is not necessarily just meanness on behalf of some grasping financial advisers, looking to work in the big end of town, where there are lots of fees. In fact, most of them are not thinking of their wallets first. Rather, they know that it is hard to get good diversification for people with smaller amounts of money unless they use managed funds. A lot of these advisers who need bigger amounts of money come from the share brokers, who use 'directs' (individual securities) rather than managed funds. This problem of getting good and proper diversification is the main reason that people with 'small' amounts ought to use multi asset class (MAC) funds (see below).

Think of it this way: if you had $200,000 to invest and you had a 10% allocation to New Zealand shares, that would mean that you would expect to have $20,000 in New Zealand shares. Other than buying into a New Zealand share fund, it would be difficult to buy enough different companies with that money: to be fully diversified in New Zealand shares you would probably need to own 10–20 different companies. You could buy small amounts of that number of companies (say, $1–2,000 each) through Sharesies or Hatch, but if you approached most of the New Zealand share brokers, they would probably have a minimum brokerage fee, which would make the transaction too expensive. Therefore, to be able to use a full-service share broker and access the research and advice that they have is usually not viable for smaller investors: they will need to either provide their own advice or invest through managed funds.

Time is money

To manage a portfolio yourself takes more than just knowledge and skill — it takes time as well. If you are thinking of looking after your own investments in retirement, I will assume you have done a self-assessment honestly, and that you have the requisite knowledge and skill. These two attributes (knowledge and skill) represent quite a high bar. Over the decades of my career, I have noticed how investment has become more (and more) complex as new investment products have been introduced and a greater range of countries and industries have become available for investment. You have to assess yourself in terms of all of the options and to make sure that you know them and can consider their value in your portfolio.

Good fund managers and financial advisers who manage their clients' investments live, eat and breathe their portfolios. This is partly an attitude (their work is important) and partly a habit — they start and continue their days doing the things that are critical to good investment management, reading the right material, talking to the right people, thinking and acting. This takes time.

It may be time that you do not have: it is easy to think that you will have the time to manage your investments when you are in retirement. If you really do, that is great. However, most commonly, people have other things that they want to do in retirement — and their partner may have plans which do not include having to stay at home while you manage your investments (one partner is suggesting jumping into the camper van and heading south for a week while the other is worried whether they will have enough connectivity so they can increase the portfolio weightings to Australian equities as planned). Investment decisions can pop up at any time and if you plan to have a busy retirement moving around the place, you might be better with a MAC fund or to have a managed account.

Knowledge, skills, attitude and habits are critical to performing any task. When it comes to investment you have to also add time to that list. Do not think of managing your money yourself unless you have them all in abundance. As I said in the introduction of this book, the investment capital that you have will be the most you will ever have, and you need to be very careful that it is well invested.

As noted previously, there are four main ways that you can invest in retirement. Each is more suitable for some, but not suitable (or sometimes not possible) for others. For example, for people with less than $250,000 it is difficult (perhaps not quite impossible) to have a managed account with a financial adviser. I set out some more detail on each below. You will note that there is much more on managed funds because most people will use managed funds to some extent, and a lot of people will use managed funds completely.

1. Managed funds

Managed funds come in a wide range of types and most are described below. They have major benefits of providing very quick and easy diversification with professional management, and they are suitable for a lot of people because they hand the problem of investment selection (choosing which investments that you will own in each of the different asset classes) to someone who knows the field.

Managed funds are about as good as the manager. In New Zealand there are some excellent managers of funds but there are also some fairly ordinary ones — choosing which to go to is difficult without independent research and that is not usually available to small investors. This is a problem that remains unsolved in New Zealand for all managed funds, including KiwiSaver.

Managed funds come in several different types: multi asset class vs single asset class, active vs passive. We also have KiwiSaver funds, which, although they are managed funds, have some of their own quite attractive features. (KiwiSaver funds are also described below.)

Managed funds are most suitable for those with 'smaller' amounts of money — up to perhaps $250,000. For these people, multi asset class funds are the most convenient — you are diversified across all asset classes as well as within each asset class. Such people struggle to be fully diversified by buying 'directs' (individual securities), and a MAC fund provides them with complete diversification in one fell swoop. MAC funds include most KiwiSaver funds and drawdown funds.

An alternate strategy could be to choose a single asset class (SAC) fund for each asset class and buy that in proportion to your required asset allocation. This is likely to mean that you will have to own six or more different funds and you will therefore have the problem of trying to choose each of these as you hope to find the best in each class. It also leads to more management.

However, you may use a SAC fund at times to give you exposure to some particularly desirable industry or investment type — for example, I own managed funds in areas like automation, robotics, medical devices and biotech and these funds give me exposure to these kinds of things without my adviser having to find the individual company that might prove best in each area (something my adviser or I would be incapable of doing without spending every waking moment studying them).

Multi asset class funds (MAC)

The first thing that most smaller investors should consider is simply to have one fund which has the right risk for you. This single fund would own all of the main asset classes (New Zealand shares, listed property, international shares, fixed interest, cash, etc.). As such it is diversified across each of the asset classes and also diversified within each asset class. Most fund managers have a range of multi asset class funds which they offer for people with different risk tolerance. They name these funds conservative, balanced, growth and aggressive, and your job is to select the one with the right amount of risk for you and then select the manager who is likely to give the best performance.

Kiwisaver

Most KiwiSaver funds are MAC funds, and we are all familiar with them. In fact, KiwiSaver is a good option for those in retirement; you can invest in a MAC fund at whatever level of risk that you can tolerate. KiwiSaver is:
- very well regulated;
- a highly competitive market, meaning they are often cheaper than other comparable funds; and
- very transparent with results of most funds published regularly by Morningstar, making comparison of performance easy.

People who are over 65 can join (or rejoin) KiwiSaver. Because they are over 65, they can then draw down on their fund whenever they like — most KiwiSaver funds allow a regular (i.e. monthly) drawdown. Because you can draw on KiwiSaver if you are over 65, your KiwiSaver fund can be a little like a bank account in its operation (although the underlying assets and risk profile is quite different). In fact, withdrawals are a little slower than bank accounts and a KiwiSaver account will not be as safe as most bank deposits. However, the higher returns from KiwiSaver make up for this and I do see KiwiSaver as a good option for retirees looking for an account to draw down from.

I can see no reason to use a standard MAC fund but would probably use a KiwiSaver or a drawdown fund by preference. This is because it is likely to be cheaper and because on all measures, KiwiSaver is the same as or better than other standard MAC managed funds.

Drawdown funds

These are also MAC funds. As I write, there is only one of these in New Zealand called the Lifetime Retirement Income Fund (I am a director, small shareholder and I have invested in the fund). This fund is a balanced fund, and it differs from KiwiSaver in that the fee you pay covers ongoing guidance regarding what your drawdown rate should be. Lifetime communicates with you each year and, taking account of the balance remaining in your account, the economic outlook, likely investment returns, your tax rate and your ever-changing age, etc., it informs you of what your safe drawdown rate should be. In my view, this is a service much needed in New Zealand, and it seems certain that we will see more of these kinds of funds in the future.

This guidance on your safe drawdown rate is a very real point of difference between drawdown funds and KiwiSaver and other MAC funds. As pointed out in the early chapters of this book, a drawdown rate should be personal and change with the times. Lifetime offers the option of a higher drawdown rate early in retirement (the 'all go' time) but, as you age (the "slow go" time) it may make a recalibration. The guidance that Lifetime provides comes from an in-house actuary and I think this feature will be highly valued by retirees using specialist drawdown funds.

Other MAC managed funds

There are other MAC managed funds which are neither KiwiSaver nor specialist drawdown funds. These are the managed funds which used to be the only option before KiwiSaver and drawdown funds came along. The banks and other investment houses have these funds with a range of risk profiles and usually with the full range of asset classes. While some of these funds give good returns, they tend to be more expensive than KiwiSaver and lack the guidance which comes from drawdown funds. Unless they come with very good performance (and some may), and are not available as KiwiSaver funds, it is difficult to see why anyone over the age of 65 would use these now as a drawdown option.

Single asset class funds (SAC)

Generally, having just one MAC fund with all of the different asset classes brought together will be what most retired people do. However, another option is to invest in a range of single asset class funds in proportions that give you the right exposures and the right amount of risk. This will require more management for you and more fund selection (which is no small thing).

SAC funds can give investment exposure to a very wide range of asset classes — shares, property, fixed interest and cash. You can buy all investment types, whether by geography (country or region) or by industry (technology, retail, energy, healthcare, etc.). You can buy into major trends (e.g. cleantech) or into areas that are likely to be key in the coming years (e.g. automation and robotics).

Selecting the right fund

Whether you are investing in a MAC (including KiwiSaver) or a bunch of SAC funds, you will need to select one(s) that are good. There has been a global trend to use passive (index tracking) funds because they are cheap. In New Zealand there has been strong guidance from the FMA (Financial Markets Authority) and others that fees are one of the biggest (perhaps they would say the biggest) factor in fund selection.

However, I beg to differ on this: although price is important when you purchase anything, so too is value (Oscar Wilde once talked about people who know the price of everything but the value of nothing).

The important thing with investment is not the price that you pay but the returns that you get after you have paid fees. Fees are important (they are clearly a component of the final returns that you will get net of fees) but they are not the sole factor for deciding.

For a given level of risk, net returns are the most important. The problem is, of course, while we can see what the returns were in the past, we do not know what they are going to be in the future. There are firms who study managed funds and advise the advisers, but these firms and their research data are prohibitively expensive for a retail investor to buy into. (As an adviser, I used to have a subscription to Morningstar research so that I could advise my clients with confidence and that cost about $2,500 each year). Morningstar does quantitative and qualitative research on managed finds — i.e. they consider past returns but also look at the people involved and the investment processes and so try to assess how good the funds are. Although there are tables for past returns of managed funds, there is no easily available qualitative assessment for managed funds at a price that retail investors could afford.

KiwiSaver funds are no different in so far as there is little qualitative research available to the public. KiwiSaver is a highly competitive market and fees tend to be lower than comparable funds that are non-KiwiSaver. Moreover, there are a number of firms that do collate return data, which they publish in various forms and make past returns easy to compare. Good places to look are:

- Morningstar quarterly survey
- interest.co.nz
- sorted.org.nz
- canstar.co.nz

Some of these give star ratings as well as their past returns (e.g. Canstar gives a star rating for features) or give an assessment of fees and services (e.g. sorted). However, there is no research that is free that rates the investment processes and the people — this is just too expensive to do to be able to give it away.

Nevertheless, the other information giving past returns is useful: if a manager has been top of the charts in a particular area (e.g. balanced funds) for 10 years, that is unlikely to be luck. Chances are this manager has done well because it has good investment processes and good people. Past performance is no guarantee of future performance, but it is an indicator of it. There are managers who have consistently led in various risk categories, and these will probably continue to do well.

Choosing on past performance may not always work but if a fund manager has a track record for a long time (e.g. 10 years), it probably has something going for it. Fund choice is difficult without detailed research, and looking at performance over a long period is probably the best that most of us can do.

Active vs passive managed funds

One decision that you will need to make is whether to invest in actively managed funds or in passive funds. Passive funds invest to follow an index (or a group of indices if it is a MAC fund). There is no research into the value of securities — a computer makes the decision and follows the index blindly. As such, passive funds expect to get the market return (less their fee). Because there are no people involved in making investment decisions, passive funds tend to be cheap.

Active managers make assessments of securities and of markets and try to outperform the market average. Active managers research what is happening and decide whether to move away from their target asset allocation because they view particular asset classes as likely to perform better or worse. They also decide which industries they like (perhaps they invest heavily in tech or healthcare) and research and choose which particular companies and securities they will own and which they will sell. All of this research and human decision-making costs money and so active fund managers cost.

There has been considerable debate regarding whether people are better off with active or passive management, much of it based on vested interest. I would make the following points regarding this area:
1. If you are building a portfolio of different SAC funds, you can choose which style you would prefer in each asset class. For example, you could have a portfolio of funds with New Zealand equities and listed property under active management, but the rest in passive management.

2. It is often said that after fees a lot of active funds do not beat the market. They don't but — but passive ones never beat the market after fees. In fact, active funds only have to beat the passive funds after their fees
3. Passive funds are sometimes very expensive in New Zealand compared to their overseas counterparts. I look at some fees on passive funds and my eyes water. Price is the only thing that passive funds have going for them, so you do want to invest in funds with low fees. They can vary greatly in cost, and this is an area where it pays to shop around.
4. Fees really matter when we look at fixed interest investments. The returns on these are currently so low that a high(ish) fee can swallow up a good bit of the return. Moreover, while there is scope for active managers to give superior returns, it is more limited in fixed interest than it is for shares.
5. There are some asset classes (especially New Zealand shares and listed property) where you should certainly invest actively. Research house and investor Mercer have done a survey every five years for the last 20 years and found consistently that the average New Zealand fund manager beats the index. This is because the New Zealand market is inefficient, under-researched and 50% of the market is owned by offshore investors who, unlike New Zealand share owners, are not trying very hard to get the very best out of their investments (many offshore investors are simply looking for some New Zealand sharemarket exposure for diversification).
6. It is much more difficult to beat international sharemarkets, and this is an area where you may well use some passive funds. The fees on passive international funds can be cheap or they can be expensive. This is a market where the product is the same and where you really want the cheap version.

I believe that most investors should have a mixture of active management and passive management according to the particular asset classes they are investing in. My main portfolio is invested as follows:

Asset class	Investment types
New Zealand shares	Active — all individual companies
Australian shares	Active — all individual companies
International shares	Active and passive — some managed funds (both active and passive) and some individual companies
Listed property	Active — some funds for Australia and international, and individual companies for New Zealand
Fixed interest	One active fund and a range of individual securities
International fixed interest	One active managed fund, no direct securities

Notes:
1. I like active management for risk management where it is possible and makes sense.
2. I am invested actively in New Zealand and Australia and remain confident that these outperform passive management. This part of the portfolio uses no managed funds.
3. International shares has some passive management for areas where it is difficult to make calls (e.g. automation/robotics, medical devices and clean energy). Most of the portfolio is either directly in individual companies or actively managed through UK investment trusts.
4. Most New Zealand fixed interest is invested in direct securities with just one actively managed fund that has performed well.
5. International fixed interest is in just one actively managed fund.

Tax on managed funds

Managed funds in New Zealand are almost always Portfolio Investment Entities (PIEs). As such, they have their own special system of tax, which is designed so that people who invest in managed funds are taxed at their own rate, rather than the rate of the managed fund. This system of taxation was introduced just before KiwiSaver started and removed a significant barrier to managed fund investment. In fact, the PIE regime means that there is now a small advantage for many people to invest in managed funds rather than directly into the markets.

As an investor in managed funds, you need to supply the fund(s) that you are investing in with your Prescribed Investor Rate (PIR), which is based on your last two years of income. There are four rates for investors: 0%, 10.5%, 17.5% and 28%. Note that the top rate of tax for a managed fund investment is 28%, which could be a considerable saving if you were on the 33% or 39% rate as an individual.

It is important that you give the correct PIR to the fund(s) that you invest in; if you give the wrong rate, you will effectively be underpaying or overpaying. When you overpay you can get a refund but if you underpay you will have to do a tax return and pay the shortfall. The IRD (or its computer) checks that you have the right PIR against the other income that you have. Provided that you have the right rate, the tax that the managed fund pays for you is a final tax and there is no need to do a tax return.

2. Going DIY

This is still an option for a few people. Although there was a time when fewer and fewer investors were doing their own thing, the advent of some new platforms (e.g. InvestNow, Hatch and Sharesies — and there will be others) has kicked DIY investing back into life. It should be noted that of the three companies mentioned above, only Hatch and Sharesies allow for direct investment into individual companies. InvestNow does provide a platform for investment but only into managed funds. (InvestNow has a suite of managed funds that you can choose from and so build your own portfolio complete from a range of MAC or SAC funds.)

The thing that these three platforms do have in common is that they do not provide advice. They provide a trustee and custodial service so that your investments can be held on a bare trust, which makes management and keeping tax records easy (this is especially important for international investments where the Foreign Investment Funds tax regime applies). They also give the ability to buy into a very wide range of companies and investment both at home and abroad (at the time of writing Hatch only offers US investments but I understand that is likely to change).

However, Sharesies, Hatch and InvestNow do not have research departments, nor are they set up to give advice. Decisions on what to buy and, just as important, what and when to sell are up to you.

As such, these platforms should really be for sophisticated investors. Although there are many younger people happily investing on these platforms (and hopefully doing well enough), I think there should be few retired investors with their total portfolios invested, and for which they have had no advice. Quite simply, as a retired investor your investment portfolio is now your means of living, and it is too important to be advice-free.

Most people who are going to run their own portfolios and do it by buying directs (individual companies on the sharemarket or the debt market) ought to be with a full-service broker, who, for the much higher brokerage fee that is charged, gives you the benefit of research and advice. There may be a few retired people who are especially interested in investment and who can successfully DIY (I know a couple), but it will be a big job and had better be a labour of love. Researching companies and securities and keeping up-to-date with the many issues regarding the investment climate is nearly a full-time job. If you want to be a fund manager, go for it; if you want to kick back and enjoy retirement, look at managed funds or a fully managed account from a financial adviser.

One thing that would be easier now compared to a few decades ago is record keeping. Financial advisers, the direct brokers and new entrants (Sharesies, Hatch, InvestNow, and whoever else might come along) have custodial platforms, which take over the record-keeping functions. These hold your investments in custody and allow you to look at your portfolio 24/7. They show the portfolio's asset allocation (a critical thing for you to watch) and the latest available price of each security. At the end of the financial year, they will provide a document which will fairly easily allow you or your accountant to do your tax return.

3. A mix of directs and funds

I think this is a better choice for a lot of people who want to DIY, and you should know it is also an approach that is often taken by many professional investors. Using managed funds, whether active of passive, for the bulk of your exposure and buying a small number of directs is a good strategy. The managed funds give you diversification, and the directs, if they are chosen well, will give you some outperformance.

Sometimes the managed funds will be used to get a wide and general exposure. For example, in the international shares class you could own a fund based on the S&P 500. This gives you excellent exposure to the 500 biggest listed companies in the US. On top of that you might buy a few direct companies that you have researched and believe will outperform (e.g. you might buy some Amazon, Nike and Pfizer).

Others may reverse this: bigger investor could own 50 different listed companies to give them reasonable diversification and exposure. Then, when they look around for things which they think will do exceptionally, they see industries that are worthy of investment — e.g. automation and robotics or genetics. It would be near to impossible to pick the winner in these areas — finding the one company that will do best in the fast-moving world of automation and robotics over the next 5 years is to look for a needle in a haystack. Better instead to buy a managed fund that is based on automation and robotics, where there are managers who are expert in the area and who spend all their time hunting in haystacks. Moreover, they will not buy just one or two companies; they will own dozens of companies. The winners are likely to be in the fund, but in any event, you will get good exposure to automation and robotics or genetics and enjoy the fruits of these burgeoning areas.

Mixing managed funds with some directs is a good option; it gives both the overall, diversified exposure and the interest (possible fun) of picking individual companies. It can suit people with a lot of money and relatively small investors. However, you still have the problem of investment selection. If you are not with an adviser, both managed funds and the directs are difficult to choose. The directs are probably of lesser importance because for most they will be smaller amounts of money. Moreover, if you are really interested you could subscribe to a 'tip sheet' to give guidance as do the retired people I know who DIY.

The choice of managed funds is still fraught. If in doubt, in most areas you are probably better going to passive funds — the one asset class where this is probably not true is in the New Zealand shares asset class, because the average fund manager beats the market. If you do go to passive funds, make sure that they are cheap (there are some that are expensive which ruins the whole point of passive funds). The choice of active funds will remain difficult whether we are talking about MAC or SAC funds. This has been (and continues to be) the case with KiwiSaver, and it will remain an area of great difficulty until (or if) advice becomes more readily available (possibly through artificial intelligence).

4. Managed accounts through financial advisers

If you have enough money, this will probably be the best means of managing investments for most retirees. Technically, this is called a Discretionary Investment Management Service (DIMS). As the name suggests, financial advisers are given your investment funds and they have discretion as to how it is invested. Effectively, financial advisers become fund managers, taking your money and investing it on your behalf in a way that has been agreed with you.

That may sound scary — handing your life savings to someone else and letting them go to it should be scary. Of course, we do that quite happily with KiwiSaver and other managed funds, but they are different in the sense that we do not see or probably even know the person who is making the investment decisions. Rest assured that having your money invested under a DIMS arrangement is very well regulated by the FMA and controlled by the firms themselves who offer it. Such arrangements are also very well documented.

It should be noted that people and firms who offer DIMS managed accounts may invest your money in a number of styles. For example, there are firms which will invest your money in a range of managed funds, whereas there are others who invest in 'directs', i.e. they buy and sell individual shares and other securities on the sharemarket. This latter group are the investment houses which have grown out of the stock broking firms (indeed, they are still members of the NZ Stock Exchange). Here I am thinking of the companies like Craigs Investment Partners, Jarden and Forsyth Barr (and some others), who between them have many billions of dollars which are managed by their teams of advisers. In fact, over the last twenty years or so, the basic business model of the share brokers has changed from buying and selling shares on behalf of their clients, to managing their clients' money through managed accounts.

Managed accounts have a number of advantages:
- The people who are managing your money know you and your goals. As such, they can tailor the portfolio to what you want and agree a drawdown rate with you.
- Many people are very close to their advisers who are managing their money. They know what the adviser is doing and the thinking that informs their decision-making.

- Many of the advisers who offer DIMS are investment specialists; this is especially so for the firms that we used to know as share brokers, who live, eat and breathe it.
- You can have influence over the way in which the money is invested. It is easy for you to require that certain industries or companies are not invested in, e.g. oil companies, gambling and other 'sin stocks'. Moreover, you can request/require that there is a heavy weighting to certain technologies of other areas that you have identified are worthy of investment.
- A managed fund means you have an adviser on call. Things happen, markets rise and fall, and it can be good to have an adviser who has got to know you and your position on hand.

In many ways managed accounts give you the best of both direct investment and professional management. They give a personal touch for your investment management, which you do not get with managed funds (you cannot call the people who make the investment decisions for your KiwiSaver account), and at the same time give professional management.

However, there are some concerns:

- A lot of people are excluded because they do not have enough money. Generally, you will need at least $250,000 to have a managed account, and in some cases $500,000 and even more for a few firms. A managed account is probably not possible if you have under $250,000 unless it is nearly all managed funds.
- The investment performance could be about as good as the individual who is doing the work. Some firms and banks have a 'house view' and everyone in the firm will have to follow this, while others will give their advisers more discretion.
- Someone could go off on a tangent and invest your money badly. This is possible with small firms but very unlikely for the bigger ones. The bigger firms have large compliance departments and set parameters within which their advisers need to stay.

People are frequently a bit nervous when they are asked to sign documents allowing financial advisers to manage their investments without recourse to you: that they can buy and sell without first asking for permission or approval. Here are some replies to this and most of them will cover the kinds of protection that are in place for you and your money:

- Your investments are held in trust in your name (this is called a bare trust). Your funds cannot be intermingled with the firm's own funds. If the firm goes broke, your money is separate.
- You can look at what is in your account online 24/7. You have access to look at your account via a password.
- Your money can only come out of your account to a bank account that has been nominated by you.
- The firms themselves set rules which their advisers have to follow, and these rules are strictly enforced. The rules are such that an adviser cannot put more than a certain percentage of your funds into any single security, they must not buy and sell frequently ('churn' in the jargon), they can only invest in approved/researched investments, and investment performance is good. The big firms, in particular, continually monitor their advisers and provide discipline.
- The firms will have to stand behind their adviser employees. If the employee is negligent and something goes badly wrong, the firm will need to make good.

You should note that some managed accounts from advisers are effectively selling their own products. These are, I think, less useful, as are the ones who limit themselves to selling solely managed funds. I am also less keen on very small firms (one or two principals) because they would have less capacity to make good a mistake and the adviser(s) are not surrounded by colleagues to talk issues through.

Generally, I prefer the bigger firms that have grown out of the share broker model; these are investment specialists that can invest in the widest range of investment types, have big compliance departments and, for the most part, have the wherewithal to stand behind mistakes from any wayward adviser. Most importantly, they have a very wide range of investments they can choose from, and the firms are steeped in research and what is going on in companies in the market.

Summary of investment choices:

Managed funds	- Good for people with small portfolios - MAC usually preferable - Difficult to choose which is best
Direct investments	- Requires expertise - Need significant money to achieve full diversification - Must ensure sufficient international exposure - Low cost
Combination managed funds and directs	- An excellent option as diversification and directs should give additional return - Need ability to pick managed funds and direct companies - Suits those with 'smaller' amounts and who have some expertise
Managed account	- Depends on finding the right person/firm - The best if you have the best person

Getting some help

Having spent about 30 years as an adviser, you would expect me to suggest that most people should get some help and take advice. Of course, this is not easy; there is always difficulty in finding just the right professional.

Financial advisers come in many different shapes and sizes, and it is hard to be general when covering such a diverse bunch. However, the basic business model for financial advisers who advise on investments is taking their clients' money and investing it for them. These investments come in nearly all of the types outlined above, with some advisers mostly filling the asset class buckets with directs and some using managing funds.

On the whole, I prefer advisers who use directs, and these come out of the specialist investment firms that we used to call share brokers (they are still members of the NZX). These people try to beat the market by selecting securities (shares and fixed interest), but they may also use some managed funds to give exposures to areas and industries that they are not expert in (e.g. biotechnology). There is a transparency about this direct model — you have a bespoke portfolio made up of companies and other securities, which means you can easily see exactly what you own.

However, there are many advisers who largely (or wholly) use managed funds. Although you are paying a fee on fees with these advisers (the adviser charges a fee and the managed funds charge fees), there are some excellent managed funds available, and a good adviser is able to identify these. By investing in these top managed finds, such advisers aim to add value beyond the scope of their fees to get you excellent investment performance. The theory is that you are paying an adviser to invest your money in the right fund and additional returns make the adviser's fees worthwhile.

In my experience, this theory can work in practice — there are some very good managed funds and a good adviser knows where to find them.

The fees that financial advisers charge are usually (but not always) a percentage of the amount that you have invested. If you have $500,000 invested and the fee is 1%, that means an annual fee of $5,000 (paid monthly). The percentage will tend to reduce as the amount of money to be invested increases: if you had $2 million to invest, the fee could be 0.75%. Rather than a percentage, some advisers have an agreed fee, although this will probably be based on the amount that you have to invest.

Fees are important and, under financial advice law and regulation, need to be disclosed properly before you invest. Fortunately, there would seem to be fewer advisers who basically sell investments on commission. This was common in the past and did lead to a sell-and-be-damned approach by some less scrupulous advisers.

Nevertheless, fees do eat into your returns, and you need to be convinced that advisers who manage your money are earning their keep; most will add value to your situation, hopefully giving you better returns but also giving peace of mind that you are not investing badly.

A part of the fee that you will pay will be for your investments to be held in trust, and for the adviser business to keep your investments in its custody. The platforms that are used for this hold the investments in your name and save considerable time in record keeping as well as allowing you to see your portfolio online at any time.

When considering advisers, you are generally looking for people who will manage your money and, as such, you will have an ongoing relationship with them. Obviously, you will have to consider their experience and judge their competency. The firm for which they work will be a large part of this. Important too is the makeup of the individual: his or her responsiveness, communication skills, character, trustworthiness, and your perception of their interest in you and your situation (compared to their own self-interest!).

A few tips which may help in adviser selection:
1. Try to find someone to invest your money a few years before retirement. There are some people through their sixties who have no cash to invest but who, when they have sold the farm or downsized the house, can suddenly invest. However, most of us have some money to invest leading up to retirement and you should find someone and get them to invest your money

as early as you can. It is better to have a dress rehearsal with a small amount of money than go straight to the main event.

2. Be ruthless if you have doubts about your adviser(s). There are lots of advisers and good people who can manage your investments. If, either when you are looking for an adviser or have appointed one, you find you have doubts, move on and find another.
3. Finding an adviser is little different from finding a hairdresser or someone to mow the lawns (although I would argue that the stakes are a bit higher when the person is going to be looking after your life savings!). Word of mouth is often the best way to find someone, although you should check carefully that the person being recommended to you is doing the same job that you need done.
4. Some people like the idea of having two portfolios, managed separately by different advisers. This has a lot to recommend it (you are, effectively, diversifying management). However, because of the way that fees are usually calculated, you are likely to pay more in fees — two relatively small portfolios would generally attract higher percentages than one larger one.
5. Negotiate the fees that are suggested by advisers. I could show many examples of people who have been able to negotiate significantly lower fees than what was originally asked.
6. Be careful of an adviser tied to just one strategy or fund manager. There are advisers who are completely wedded to the way they invest and will hear of no other strategy or method. No single way of investment stands out as much better than the rest — if it really was so much better, we would all be doing it.
7. Financial advice is now very well regulated. Financial advice was first regulated in 2011, and then re-regulated in 2020. People who receive advice from a financial adviser can have confidence that the advice will be reasonably good. There will, however, still be instances of poor advice — every industry

and profession from accounting, law, medicine, engineering, etc. has some bad eggs, and financial advice is no exception. However, there is less likelihood of some of the worst cases of dishonesty or incompetence that have been seen in the past.
8. Last but not least, trust is perhaps the most important criterion; this means trust not just of the individuals, but also trust of the firms they work for. Trust is made up of personal qualities along with the way advisers get paid. How long the advisers and their firms have been around is also important. Ultimately, these individuals and the firms they work for will know a lot about you — you have to feel comfortable when you share that information.

Most people need some advice. I hope this book is useful and allows you to settle some issues. However, useful though I hope it is, no book can take the place of good advice that is personalised to you. Finance and investment form a big body of knowledge and, while there are some immutable principles, there is certainly a lot of change which is on-going.

In retirement you take on the role of money manager. The capital that you have will most likely be a significant, even critical part of your income and, therefore, your wellbeing in retirement. A good, trusted adviser ought to be a critical part of this.

> **I reckon #10 — Think about getting someone else to manage your money**
> I have a financial adviser. I know a fair bit about money management and about investment but, even so, I have someone who invests my money for me.
> In 2020 I had a good look at my finances and myself. I first considered how I had been doing as an investor. I measured my performance against other balanced investors that I know and decided that I was doing all right — not spectacularly good but not bad either. Considering the risk I was taking, I was doing OK.

However, when I looked at my portfolio, I saw that there were investments that I should have sold long ago — there was certainly a bit of dross that had been there for a good while, providing a drag on investment performance. When I thought about this, I knew what was happening: I get quite attached emotionally to my investments and do not easily sell them. I am not ruthless and hold on to investments beyond their use-by. I decided that I was quite good at identifying good companies and buying them, but not so good at selling.

Moreover, I have always been quite busy and do not give my own investments the priority they deserve. I tend to look at my own investments in the evening or some other dead time instead of devoting an hour or so of my best time. I do not prioritise my own money (the cobler's family is the poorest shod).

And so, struggling a bit with the idea of giving up a lifetime of managing my own investments, I have handed a part over to a financial adviser to manage. When I did this, I promised myself that I would not interfere (and on the whole I have done a pretty good job at just letting go and leaving him to it even though I look at the portfolio online most days).

It has worked out well: although there are always investments that I would like to see in the portfolio, I am getting better returns. There is a much more dispassionate approach to the portfolio than I could ever manage with my own money — someone who spends all day, every day looking at a screen does better than I could have managed with my part-time approach.

I feel very happy with what has happened with my investment and, although I will always watch over my investments and, perhaps, interfere if I felt very strongly about something, I doubt that I will manage my own investments again.

Afterword

Writing a book means learning. There should, of course, be some learning for the reader, but what you should realise is that there is also learning for the writer. Well, this writer, anyway.

I have just finished my second proofread and I am about to hit the SEND button so that this will go to the publishers. As I have read and corrected, I realised that from the time I started writing to now a few months later, my thinking has subtly changed.

The two things that were most heavily underlined for me were how difficult it is to look after your savings and turn them into an income, and how important it is that it's done properly. I have always known this — I started the book with a (nearly) true story about a couple who woke up to find they had $7,595,777.43 in their bank account and whose predominant emotion was fear. You would think a nest egg that big would inspire joy, but I have long known the reality that large amounts create anxiety instead. Nevertheless, spending some months at a keyboard researching, writing, thinking and remembering the people I have helped with their investments has confirmed for me how difficult it is to raid the nest egg.

The fear of loss is much stronger than the hope of profit, and, quite rightly, that fear of loss grows as we age.

Two other things came through strongly while I was writing: first, setting a drawdown rate is hard. Over the months I have been writing this book, I have frequently asked retired (or near retired) friends how they know how much they can spend from a given amount of capital. No one answered that they would use the 4% rule or the 6% rule — in fact, no one ever talked about using any rule of thumb; I cannot say that I ever really got an answer that could constitute a plan (other than some people who had done quite elaborate spreadsheets). If actuaries and other experts in this field can argue amongst themselves, how hard is it for the rest of us to decide on a rate to draw on our capital that will give a good life and last long enough?

Second, investment is no easy matter at the best of times, and retirement is a time when the stakes are highest, and the process at its most difficult. Over the years I have gradually moved away from the idea that DIY was a good option for retired people's investments and now think that there are very few who should satisfactorily do this. I know it is hard for those with smaller amounts of money to get good advice, but I do think that selecting one or two managed funds is preferable to DIY.

Retirement should be the time of your life and not be clouded with worry about money. You will always have to be vigilant, but I know that a good retirement is more likely when you choose an adviser and firm that you trust, rather than trying to select and manage your investments yourself.

Glossary

There are some important terms that I use a great deal in this book, which I have summarised here for quick explanation. They are:
1. Diversified portfolio
2. Asset allocation
3. Listed property
4. Drawdown rate
5. Net worth

Diversified portfolio

Although most people think they know what a diversified portfolio is, I know of plenty of instances where people have used the word 'diversified' and only got it half right. A very good example of this was in 2009 when the Global Financial Crisis (GFC) was casting very dark shadows over economies and investment markets, and when most finance companies were going broke. Many times, I heard people say something like: 'I thought I was well diversified — I had my money in five different finance companies.'

Well, these people were half right: they had diversified within the investment type (i.e. finance companies) but they had not diversified outside finance companies. These mostly retired people (and there were quite a lot of them) had not spread their cash around a range of different investment types — they did not own shares, they did not own listed property, they did not own

investments outside of New Zealand, etc.
And so, they had done half the job.
A properly diversified portfolio has two features:
1. **It has exposure to all of the main asset classes.** This means there are investments in each of:
   - shares
   - listed property
   - fixed interest
   - cash

   These are the four main investment types (often called asset classes) and, as I explained in the second part of this book, each investment type gives a different investment performance depending on the prevailing economic weather at any time. Having some of each of these four investment types means that regardless of how the economy is performing (boom times, recession, inflation, deflation, etc.), you should have at least one investment type that is doing well. Of course, each of these four main investment types can be further broken down, e.g. shares can be broken down to NZ shares, global shares, emerging market shares, and can be further broken down by industry (tech shares, healthcare shares, etc.).
2. **The holdings within each asset class are well diversified.** Not only do you need exposure to each of the four main investment types, but within each of the main types, you need multiple different individual investments. For example, within the shares investment type, it would not do to have just one company's shares — this could have been shares in Amazon (which would have given you a stunningly good performance) but it also could have been CBL Insurance (which went broke). Diversification within each investment type takes out this hit-or-miss gamble — you need to be exposed to dozens of companies both at home and abroad.

All retired people with money should have it invested in a properly diversified portfolio. You can do this in a number of ways:

1. You could simply buy a fund that is fully diversified as it holds a wide range of securities in each investment type. This is called a 'multi asset class' fund. You could have your money held in this and arrange a regular drawdown (probably fortnightly).
2. You could use a KiwiSaver fund. Over 65s can join KiwiSaver and could use it to hold their investments. Most funds will allow regular withdrawals. For over 65s (who have the right to withdraw at any time), KiwiSaver is similar to the funds described above (i.e. multi asset class) but may have the advantage of being cheaper than comparable non-KiwiSaver funds.
3. You could use a 'drawdown fund'. There is only one of these in New Zealand at the time of writing (it is called Lifetime Retirement Income and, by way of disclosure, I have a shareholding in it). These funds are becoming popular overseas and are specially designed for retired people and come with good diversification.
4. You could go to a financial adviser who could build you a portfolio made up of a series of managed funds, each of which gives exposure to a certain investment type. This means that you would have a fund (or two) that is based on shares, a fund (or two) based on fixed interest, etc. The financial adviser would know which are the best funds in each investment type, monitor performance and make changes when necessary (for a fee).
5. You could use an investment adviser from one of the big brokerage houses who would build a portfolio by buying securities in each of the investment types: for example, they may buy 15 New Zealand companies, 50 global companies, 20 New Zealand fixed interest securities, etc. They will work this to a plan so that you have plenty of diversification and your asset allocation is as it should be.

6. You could 'do it yourself'. The DIY approach has become less common for retired people as the investment world has become more open and many investment options have developed. DIY investors need to be very careful to ensure they are properly diversified, i.e. that they have some exposure to all asset classes and that they have many different securities with each investment type.

The beauty of a diversified portfolio in retirement is that you will never lose all your money. A diversified portfolio will have exposure to hundreds (possibly thousands) of different companies and other entities, and a similar number of different securities. If all of these go broke and have no value, the world is in a huge amount of trouble. The chances are if Nike, Fisher and Paykel, General Electric, Mainfreight, Amazon, Apple, McDonalds, Contact Energy and hundreds or thousands of others have all disappeared in a puff of smoke, the value of your investments are probably the least of your problems.

On the other hand, an investment (or a few investments that are all in the same asset class) could potentially lose all their value. For example, if you had all your money in a bank or in a rental property, they could in fact go broke and take all your money with them.

Diversifying moves the risk from absolute loss (i.e. you lose all of your money) to volatility (the value of your portfolio going up and down but the great majority of your holdings remain intact though they may be worth less for a period of time). For a retired person, volatility is far preferable — we can cope with some ups and downs; we cannot cope with absolute loss.

Asset allocation

Asset allocation is the way that you mix the main investment types. In effect, it is the amount of each investment type you have in your portfolio. If you agree that an investor ought to always have something in each investment type, the next question is how much of each one are you going to have. It is unlikely that you would have equal amounts of shares, listed property and cash; instead, you will usually have a mixture that reflects the level of risk you are comfortable with.

The problem with having a view of the future is that you never really know whether it will be right. If you had a fully functioning crystal ball (with freshly charged batteries) that showed with absolute certainty that we were going to have boom times and that shares were going to do extremely well, you would allocate all of your money to that single investment type (i.e. you would be 100% invested in shares).

However, in reality, no one can ever be certain they know the future — prediction is hard. And so, we have some doubt and hedge our bets: we have a bit of everything, some exposure to all investment types as a kind of insurance policy in case the crystal ball is wrong.

Of course, the more we have in shares and listed property in a portfolio, the better returns that we will get in the long term, but also the more risk of volatility we will suffer. Shares and listed property give good returns — but they come with greater risk. Investors are continually balancing risk and return as they try to get good returns while still managing the risk involved.

As a matter of convention, most people use descriptors of portfolios (like conservative, balanced, growth) according to how much shares and listed property they have compared to how much fixed interest and cash they have. These names are just shorthand for the asset allocation of the fund — they are not formal terms, but they have grown to be common usage. You need to remember that they really describe asset allocation.

It is useful to combine growth investments (the ones where you effectively own the businesses or properties, i.e. shares and listed property) with income investments (investments where you lend your money to some entity and earn interest, i.e. fixed interest and cash). Income investments reduce the risk in portfolios and are very useful when times get bad.

The names of portfolios and the approximate asset allocations they might have are:

Name	Growth investment	Income investment	Total
Conservative	30%	70%	100%
Balanced	50%	50%	100%
Growth	75%	25%	100%

Generally, a retired investor would be likely to have a balanced portfolio (50/50) or a conservative portfolio (30/70). This is because most retired people are dependent on their portfolios for income and cannot, therefore, tolerate much risk. It has been shown very clearly that the greatest determinant of risk within a portfolio or a fund is the way that cash is allocated to the different investment types. It may be tempting to load up on shares and listed property to get more return but the increased volatility that comes with more shares may be too much to handle.

Listed property

If I was only ever allowed to invest in just one investment type, I would nominate commercial property (especially industrial). I hope that I never have to choose — I prefer to remain well diversified because there is no single investment type that does well in all economic seasons. However, I am talking up commercial property like this because I want to show how much I like that asset class (perhaps especially for retired investors).

However, I am not going to go out in the market and try to buy my own commercial property. If I did that it would be a big slug of money for me and leave little room for further diversification into other excellent investments. And even though it would be a lot of money for me, by commercial property standards it would be a low value property. Even if I spent $2 million, it would probably be poorly located, an older building, leased to an ordinary tenant, for quite a short term.

When it comes to investment, I do not want something ordinary — I want the best buildings, leased to the best tenants, sitting nicely in the best locations. I want it all.

So, rather than going out and buying something ordinary, I would rather get my exposure through property funds — I would rather own a small sliver of something great than own 100% of something ordinary.

I think the best property funds are the listed property vehicles. There are about 10 big funds that own large amounts of commercial property. Some names may be familiar: Precinct Property, Kiwi Property Group, Property for Industry, Goodman.

Effectively these funds buy property with shareholders' funds and some debt (usually around 35% LVR). They manage the property, bring in the rents, pay themselves a management fee, pay interest and other costs and pass the surplus onto shareholders by way of dividend. As I write, the dividend yield for listed property funds is on average about 4% (which at a time when it is hard to get 1% on a term deposit is not too bad).

Importantly, the shares of the property funds are listed on the sharemarket. This means that you can buy and sell shares, which gives the benefit of liquidity. However, being listed does mean volatility. Like all companies listed on the sharemarket, the shares of property funds do move up and down quite a lot. Mostly the share price should reflect the value of the underlying properties but the sharemarket can have a mind of its own and can be very volatile. The shares for property funds can move around quite a lot, especially responding to interest rate movements (lower interest rates are good for property funds because low interest costs increase profits and because many investors use property funds as a substitute for fixed interest when they are looking for income).

I think listed property is an excellent investment type for retirement income. This is because:
- They tend to own the very best property — near-new buildings in excellent locations leased to top tenants with long leases.
- They provide good income (usually significantly above fixed interest).
- You get both income growth and capital growth.
- They are liquid — unlike property syndicates, you can buy and sell at any time.
- You get diversification — some of the funds own dozens of properties leased to hundreds of tenants.
- They are well regulated by both the Financial Markets Authority and the NZX.
- They allow you to buy into the different types of commercial property — for example, Property for Industry owns industrial property (warehouses and the likes) while Precinct Property owns mostly office buildings.

Yes, you do have to put up with the volatility — the price is available constantly and prices can move around a lot. (This volatility can be a good thing as it can allow you to buy bargains. For example, during the GFC, I bought Goodman shares at a price which gave me a 14% dividend yield.)

When I think, talk or write of investment property, I am usually thinking of listed property. Usually these are in New Zealand but there are about 40 listed property funds in Australia and many more available around the globe.

With their diversification, good yields and liquidity, I am not sure why a retired investor would own any other sort of investment property.

Drawdown rate

The drawdown rate is the amount that you can take out (draw down) from a portfolio during your retirement. Whatever amount that you have saved for retirement or have received from the sale of a business, farm or rental properties, you will need to determine how much you can withdraw each year to live on without the money (your capital) running out before you do.

This amount is usually expressed as a percentage of the investment capital that you have at the start of your retirement. For example, the most common drawdown rate is 4%. This means that in each year of retirement you could draw down 4% of the initial amount you had when you started retirement — if you went into retirement with $500,000, you could draw $20,000 every year while you are in retirement.

Calculating the rate at which you can take money from your investments is no easy thing: there are variables like how long you will live, investment returns and inflation, which need to be estimated and brought into the calculations as assumptions. Your assessment of these variables may not prove to be correct (and therefore your drawdown rate may be incorrect). Nevertheless, experts have calculated various drawdown rates and they provide them as rules of thumb. In my view, it is much better to use one of these rules of thumb rather than to take a guess and, effectively, fly blind.

Net worth

This is not a difficult process or calculation — nevertheless, it is a most important one: it tells you what you have, how rich you are. As such, writing down the things that you own and what you owe (if anything) is effectively a stocktake and sets out the pieces on the board that you have to play with.

To do your net worth, you simply add up the value of the things that you own (house, investments, KiwiSaver, bank deposits, rental property, business, etc.) and subtract from that number the value of any debt that you have (hopefully none — see below).

In effect, you are writing down the things you own and valuing them to get a total amount you are worth. In other words, if you sold everything and paid off any debt, this would be the amount you would have available.

It is a useful thing to do because retirement is a time of life which will almost certainly represent a pivot. By this I mean that if you want, you could move into an entirely different life — you no longer have work commitments and you are now free to do whatever you want. One way or another, retirement is likely to be a different life from anything that has gone before, and you need to know and consider every resource you have.

This means that you put everything on the table — many people design a whole new life. You could (if you want) sell the house to live in a house bus, or move to Hokitika. Most people will not want to do anything too radical (we are often quite rightly tied to friends, family and the community), but if there is something that you have always hankered for, now is the time to do it.

Doing a net worth statement lets you see what you have to work with. You can sell things to buy others if you want or stay much the same as you are. The net worth statement lets you see what options you have.

As noted above this usually comes down to having a house to live in and some money to generate an income. To know this, you need to write down what you have now.

There are a few basic principles that I follow doing a net worth statement:
1. Use values that are on the conservative side of realistic. There is no point in inflating values; inflating values may give you a big number, which may make you feel good, but it will not give you a better lifestyle.
2. Be especially careful on the value you use if you own a business, farm or rental properties. Small businesses are notoriously difficult to value, and houses and farms can

sometimes also be difficult to value. However, these may make up a big proportion of your net worth and are, therefore, critical to value. If you are likely to sell property, a farm or the business, and are in doubt about their value, take some advice. You could get an estimate from real estate agents, but if you do, you should discount their value by about 10% — this is to make up for their fees and for the fact that they are frequently over-optimistic. If the value is really important to your plans (and it often is) get a registered valuation.

3. Use net values. This means reducing the value of things like your house, farm, rental property or business to account for real estate agent fees and other costs. Remember that there may be tax implications when you sell — you may have depreciation recovered or hit the 'Brightline test'.

4. Do not count things like furniture or cars. These are value losers, and, at any rate you are going to continue to own them (or something similar). They are not usually 'in play'. Although you may think that you could sell one of the cars and make do with one (in which case you would include the value of the car to be sold as a part of your net worth), generally you will own a car through nearly all of retirement and the value of it will never be included in capital to be invested.

Index

Asset allocation 78, **123-152**, 183-185
    Growth assets **123-124**, 139-140
    Income assets **123-124**, 130-139
    Tactical Asset Allocation 125
    Asset classes 139-152

Bank deposits, for retirement savings 11, **58-59**, 148

Defined benefit superannuation schemes 9, 10
Defined contribution superannuation schemes 10
Delaying retirement **38-39**, 79
Diversified portfolio 69, **180-183**
DIY investing 155, **165-168**, 178
Dollar cost averaging 67-68
Drawdown rates 70, **76-95**, 188
    Personalising **80**, 85
    The 4% Rule 71, **83-87**
    The 6% Rule 82-83, **87-88**
    The Fixed Date Rule 89-90
    Life Expectancy Rule 90-91
    Drawdown funds 93, **158-159**

Financial advisers (including selection) 154, **168-177**

Healthcare expenditure **50-51**, 53-54
House, the 106-119
    Downsizing 107-115
    Retirement villages 112-114
    Reverse mortgages 116-118
    House as income 115-118
    Selling up and renting 119

Income investments **72-73**, 184
Investment portfolios 78, **123-137**, 185
    Critical requirements 68-70
    Balanced fund 55, **69**, 185
    Conservative fund **123**, 185
    Growth fund 79, **124**, 185
    Expected returns 127
    Risk tolerance 131-137
Investment risk 125

KiwiSaver **156-158**, 161

Lake of cash 23, **64-65**

Listed property 68, **147**, 185-187

Managed funds 153, **156-165**
    Multi Asset Class Funds 153, **157-159**
    Single Asset Class Funds 153, **160-162**
    Active vs Passive Funds 162-164
    Tax on managed funds 165
Market crashes 66, **143**
Micro-business 103

Net worth 29-32, 188-190
NZ Super 75, **98-100**

Property syndicates 68

Rental property as investment 69, **73**-74
Retirement villages 112-114
Reverse mortgage 116-118
Sequencing risk 65-66

Spending capital 60-63
Spending in retirement 43-57
    All Go 44, **46-48**
    Slow Go 44, **48-49**
    No Go 44, **49-50**
    Spending categories 53-54

Three stages of retirement 44

Volatility risk 63, **126-127**

Working in retirement 101-103

I reckon # 1: Ease your way into retirement 25
I reckon # 2: Retirement is about more than the money stuff 42
I reckon #3: That old 'should I keep my health insurance' chestnut 57
I reckon # 4: Be prepared for inflation 75
I reckon #5: Keep an eye on your expenditure 95
I reckon #6: Assess the benefits of continuing to work 105
I reckon #7: Avoid selling the house and renting 119
I reckon #8: Planning is key 138
I reckon #9: Keep your portfolio simple 152
I reckon #10: Think about getting someone else to manage your money 176

Example: Working out the amount you have for investing 32
Example: The effect of part-time work post retirement 40
Example: The jam jar approach to categorising expenses 53